The Dinner Diaries

. . . .

Raising Whole Wheat Kids in a White Bread World

by Betsy Block

ALGONQUIN BOOKS OF CHAPEL HILL   2008

Published by
Algonquin Books of Chapel Hill
Post Office Box 2225
Chapel Hill, North Carolina 27515-2225

a division of
Workman Publishing
225 Varick Street
New York, New York 10014

✪ Printed on recycled stock with 30% post-consumer content.

Library of Congress Cataloging-in-Publication Data
Block, Betsy.
The dinner diaries : raising whole wheat kids
in a white bread world / by Betsy Block.
p. cm.
1. Children — Nutrition. 2. Food preferences in children.
I. Title.
RJ206.B56 2008
618.92′398 — dc22   2008009310

10 9 8 7 6 5 4 3 2 1
First Edition

Maya and Zack:
You are my sun and moon.
I just didn't know your orbit would involve so many crumbs.

Andy:
Twenty years later and we're still laughing.
What more can I say.

Ask your child what he wants for dinner only if he's buying.

—FRAN LEBOWITZ

A smiling face is half the meal.

—LATVIAN PROVERB

Words of wisdom from my grandfather: "Take your time and enjoy it."

—ELLIS BLOCK, AKA POPPY,
A GUY WHO LOVED BOTH DINNER AND LIFE

Contents

. . . .

The Dinner Diaries

. . . .

Food Fight

Maya comes upstairs Sunday morning to interrupt my meditation. "Mommy, Mommy, I have good news," she tells me excitedly. "Zack likes fried cheese!" She thinks this is good news because Zack is the only one in the family who doesn't like cheese, and that complicates things sometimes, as if life wasn't already complicated enough. He wouldn't eat pizza until he was seven, and while I can't say this kept me up at night, it did make for some awkward moments at birthday parties.

So, trying to stay in the meditative moment, I sigh, get out of bed because I meditate lying down under the covers — "I think they used to call that a nap," my husband, Andy, says — and come downstairs to find Zack sprinkling shredded cheese into an oiled pan until it comes together in a greasy, brown-edged clump. "Aren't you happy I like healthy, delicious fried cheese, Mom?" he taunts, then laughs wickedly. I shake my head and walk away; otherwise, I might do something I'll regret, like pick up the plate and dump its contents into the sink.

I'd always thought food was pretty straightforward: you're hungry, you eat; you're not, you don't. Then I became a mother.

Once we had Zack ten years ago, we quickly learned that children are constantly hungry. They need to eat every two hours around the clock in the beginning; over time that amped up to every hour in our house, although thankfully, now it's mostly when the sun is up. In fact, the word *mamma* and its ilk (*mom, mama, mommy*) derives from *mammal,* or *mammary;* in other words, someone whose primary purpose is to feed her young.

Andy and I never knew we could be engaged in this much shopping, stirring, pouring, serving, and cleaning up, all to the tune of our children's mysterious and ever-changing dietary quirks: Just because they begged us to buy it yesterday doesn't mean they'll eat it today. Just because they're hungry doesn't mean they'll eat. The constant feeding of fussy eaters, even if they're small, lovable, and closely related, takes a toll.

As is true for all of us, I started motherhood with the best intentions, but what I learned while trying to uphold the highest possible parenting standards is that if you want to stay sane, you probably shouldn't listen to experts too carefully; while many of them do indeed dole out good advice, they usually do so while holed up in clean, quiet, *child-free* offices. Meanwhile, those of us in the trenches can end up feeling like failures because our kids don't like whole wheat; they'll only eat white. And really, they'd prefer Pop-Tarts.

I suppose it's not surprising, then, that sometimes I think of the kitchen as a boxing ring, only there isn't just one opponent in the ring with us health-conscious parents; there are many more.

In this corner are the nutritionists, fists up, telling us to expand our offerings of fruits and vegetables; serve more whole grains and fish; and cut down on white bread, bad fats, and meat.

In that corner stand the slow food types, telling us to eat locally and in season, which obviously rules out most of what the nutritionists advised. This faction includes the environmentalists.

You can spot the ethicists in a third corner, index fingers jabbing the air as they go on about factory farming. The vegans, who are itching to throw some punches of their own, weren't invited into the ring. Next time.

Over here are the short but loud nonstop eaters, turning up their noses at all options, whether nutritional, sustainable, or ethical. They're just clamoring for more candy, please. ("But we said 'please'!") They're joined by other, "nicer" adults who actually do serve Pop-Tarts for a snack and who don't understand what all the fuss is about.

And in the middle of the mat? One poor mom, knocked out from exhaustion. She knows it's her job to be a limit-setting naysayer, but secretly she's a pleasure-seeking hedonist. She's the one always suggesting dinner out at the last minute, because she can't deal with cleaning up yet again. And no, she doesn't mean at a fast-food restaurant. She wants a decent meal that everyone will eat, although all she *really* wants is for the fighting to stop, please God.

She knows it could, if she'd just give into her kids' every edible desire. Lots of parents do, and why not? It makes life so much easier — at least in the short term. Besides, would it really be so wrong? And wouldn't everyone be happier that way? Just the thought of all that familial peace makes me sleepy and acquiescent. But then I'm snapped awake by the realization that millions of American children are obese or overweight, too many more are hungry, and thanks to the prevalence and low cost of junk food, children can suffer from both obesity and malnutrition at the same time. Our collective eating habits have officially become a national crisis.

No, now's not the time to give up the good fight. Instead, it's time to take it to the next level.

ONWARD AND UPWARD

"You're trying to make us more healthy, Mommy," five-year-old Maya accuses me with a pout one day.

She's right, I am. But once I set my sights on the end result — a better diet — it didn't take long to realize there's no way I can make this almost-impossible dream come true on my own. I need help. It turns out that motherhood is a team sport. In an effort to feed my family better, the time has come to call on nutritionists, chefs, farmers, scientists, food historians, and anyone else who can help me meet this elusive goal. I'm hoping these kind strangers can offer sage advice, a different perspective, and maybe even a shoulder to cry on, or braise.

In addition to all these experts, I know I also need to win Andy over to my side, which won't be easy, both because he is an exceptionally picky eater and because he doesn't really care about nutrition. He thinks I'm a little too intense about mealtime, and a thousand other things. But if we can work our way through this marital thicket and come out the other side holding hands, if we can reach a compromise and create a harmonious meal plan despite our differences, won't we be creating one teeny-tiny corner of peace in a planet gone mad? It might not matter on a global scale, but this way at least we won't be adding to the world's woes. Besides, you have to start somewhere. Why not with food? It's realistic, it's here and now, and it's a problem — at least for me; everyone else seems pretty happy with the white bread–chicken breast–broccoli status quo.

There's something else: I lie to my kids about food. I've even been known to order a cup of hot fudge to go in an ice-cream shop — "In a bag, if you have one" — then tuck it behind the milk on the top shelf of the fridge. Meanwhile, the kids think I "don't like dessert." Why do I lie like this? Because it's far easier than having to explain things all the time. So as long as I'm shooting for the moon, I might as well mention that I want to stop lying to the kids, because I'm pretty sure that Zack is onto my sneaky ways. I can't have him entering his teen years thinking his mom is a fraud. And being right.

In other words, I'm going for no less than an all-family meal makeover. That's a tall order, and to make matters worse, we're starting off in a very bad place: it's Halloween. For a mom who wants her kids to eat better, there's nothing spookier.

Chapter 1

Expert Advice

A DIFFERENT WAY

A very short farmer is sitting on a stool at the butcher-block table in the kitchen, eating dinner. She has pigtails, overalls, and a black mustache that's getting licked off. Her plate contains exactly five kalamata olives and a small pile of bread that's been cut into cubes in the hope that because it looks cute, she will actually chew and swallow it.

Normally I'd be tempted to fight with my little farmer over this meager pre-trick-or-treating meal, but this year I've promised Andy I'll take a different approach to Halloween. I figure that maybe the kids are completely obsessed with candy for the entire month of November because by stingily allowing them only one piece a day, I unintentionally enhance its appeal. Maybe if I fling the door to sugar wide open and let them have as much as they want whenever they want it, they'll feel more ownership of their lives and their bodies. Then they'll come to understand that eating well is its own reward; perhaps a meal makeover won't even be necessary.

Or maybe they'll just make themselves sick. Really, anything could happen.

I mean it. A decade into motherhood, I know all too well how

Halloween Tricks

Halloween is a conundrum—there's no way around it. So in the spirit of no escape, here are a few ideas on how to reduce the excess:

- "Ghost" neighbors who don't have kids—leave a nicely wrapped, small bag of candy on their doorstep along with a homemade card.

- Trade candy for small toys (I wish you good luck; this has never worked in our house). Next Halloween I'm taking this tactic up a level: I'm inviting a bunch of families over and setting up a store of small, cheap toys that kids can buy using candy as money.

- With older kids, cut to the chase and just buy their candy outright. This has never worked for us either; our bids have never been high enough, apparently, but next year Zack might be more interested in money than he is in candy.

- Take some of the candy into the office, church, temple, or wherever (although this too is kind of dirty pool).

- Personally, I prefer to be rid of the candy within a week at the most; I'd rather let the kids make themselves sick than have it drag on for a month or more. I also recommend pilfering some and throwing it away, unless your kids take a piece-by-piece inventory as mine do.

bad food happens to good people: the kids constantly beg for junk, I tirelessly shoot down their requests, but then somehow, they manage to beg, borrow, or steal what they're hankering for anyway. In part, this is because with Zack at the helm of the children's brigade, they've come up with a number of different strategies to wear me down. As for Andy, he doesn't need his will to be eroded; he's a much easier mark to begin with.

There's not one cataclysmic episode that illustrates the ongoing struggle between darkness and light, candy and kale; instead, there is a series of them. Take the morning I found four chocolate chips strewn on the counter. They'd been carelessly left behind by a sneak who's tall enough to reach the chips but who isn't savvy enough yet to know he has to hide the evidence. I confronted Zack. "Did you, by any chance . . ." With an embarrassed grin he asked, "How'd you know?" I gave him a scowl and a finger wag; I told him that as his mother I will always be able to sniff him out, in case he gets any more bright ideas. I hope he believed me.

Filching isn't Zack's only line of attack. He has also mastered the in-your-face approach, where we'll be grocery shopping and he'll just boldly plunk, say, a carton of lemonade in the cart without asking for permission first. Andy, as ever the one willing to take the path of least resistance, shrugs and keeps moving forward; then again, he likes lemonade as much as the next kid. As for me, I really have no problem telling Zack to put the carton back on the shelf, even if he shoots me dirty looks and starts to make a scene when I do. I have nerves of steel when it comes to my children's health and eating habits.

But I need more than that to stop Zack, because he has even more tricks up his sleeve — for example, the devious but brilliant avoidance technique that he used just a few days ago when he went to New Hampshire for a night with my dad. While they were still driving there, Zack called home on Dad's cell phone.

A few minutes ago, he told me excitedly, he was feeling a little carsick, so they pulled over to a rest stop to get something to settle his stomach.

They went inside where, he said, "Mom, they had the *best deal ever.* You can get sixty-four ounces of Coke for just ninety-nine cents!" He then added that the next time he goes to New Hampshire, he's taking along a cooler and twenty bucks. He plans on setting up a stand where he'll divide the soda into cups and sell them for two bucks a pop. "I like the way he thinks," Andy said thoughtfully when I related this story. "You're not helping anything," I coolly replied.

As for Maya — agreeable, wonderful little Maya — she's so much more cooperative than Zack that getting her to eat better than him would be a breeze, except for one small factor: she's apprenticed herself to her big brother since day one. As a result, she's been able to coerce all sorts of rubbish from us much earlier than Zack ever could, even though she has many fewer ploys, just two, really — crying and being intrinsically adorable — but both of these are Andy's downfall. For example, while Zack was in the car driving north with my dad, Andy and I whisked Maya off on errands. After our first farm-stand stop, Andy said he needed (not wanted) coffee from Dunkin' Donuts. When she heard this, Maya started in. "Mama?" she said sweetly. "Can I get one, one, one munchkin? Because anytime I see Dunkin' Donuts I just want one thing — a smoothie or a munchkin."

Of course she really wanted more than one; she just knows from past experience that shooting low is more likely to result in success. I would have said no without a second's hesitation, but Andy looked at me and mouthed, "Just one?" I tilted my head and gave him a tired nod. "Mmm, sugar high!" Maya joked when she was done with her one little munchkin. "Just kidding," she quickly clarified. Even at this tender age she already appreciates that she doesn't want to supply the enemy — me — with any more ammunition against sugar than I already have.

Speaking of sugar, by dawn's early light on the morning after Halloween, Zack and Maya are ready to get this party started. "Can we each have one *tiny* piece of candy?" Maya asks cautiously. She's expecting the usual nay-saying, candy-hating mom to hiss back "No!" Instead, much to her surprise, I brightly answer, "You can have as much as you want." I don't even follow it up with, "It's your teeth" or "Remember, you're seeing the dentist later this month."

As I said, I'm conducting an experiment to see if it's really necessary to crack down on the kids so much anymore. I obviously talk to them (okay, lecture them) about healthy eating all the time; they must have digested at least some of the information by now. Luckily, we'll be able to find out, because today, November 1, there is no school. Normally I would be bitter about this sneaky move by the teachers' union, but this year I figure it will give me a chance to see whether if I modify my behavior, the kids will spontaneously meet me halfway. If I'm not badgering them, they'll surely make good choices at least some of the time. Right?

Five minutes after they've started their binge, Zack comes over with a bag he's put together just for me, featuring lots of chocolate. This is a seriously loving gesture because he's included some of his favorite brands. "Do you mind if I save it for later?" I ask politely. It's now 7:35 a.m.

"No, no, not at all. It's yours; eat it when you want."

I can't help noticing that things are unusually civil this morning.

When he's done eating his "breakfast," he goes down to the basement, unasked, to practice his drums. Meanwhile, Maya's in the other room singing, "Mommy, I love my mommy." And now I'm telling Zack not only to brush his teeth but also to empty the dishwasher.

All my demands are met with friendly acquiescence. The kids have shared candy with both me and each other, and there is no fighting in the house. Forgetting about cavities for a minute, which is hard because Zack has eight fillings, I allow myself to wonder, Could the path to family harmony be paved with sugar?

Then again, while it's true we're all having a great day, I have the answer. By 3:30 p.m., both Zack and Maya are looking pale. "I never want to eat candy again," Zack moans, and together we realize that other than sweets, he's eaten exactly one-half of a chicken breast today.

So this is what happens when I let go.

EYES ON THE PRIZE

Food was not nearly this complicated when Zack was born. Obviously, nursing was a no-brainer. But once we hit the uneven terrain of solid foods, we lost our footing. How could we get our baby to eat nutritious veggies? What should we do when he spits out the fiber-rich whole grain bread? And why is he turning orange? (That's when we learned that there really can be too much of a good thing — at least when it comes to babies and squash.)

Feeding our firstborn was taking a little more energy than we had; I wondered if motherhood itself was intrinsically unsustainable. Soon enough, though, we got distracted by crawling, walking, and potty training. Years went by; Zack learned both how to ask for potato chips and how to cry when he didn't get them. By the time he was in kindergarten, he was on the verge of being overweight. As our beloved pediatrician Rick Goldstein asked questions about our family diet, it didn't take long for him to realize that Zack was gorging himself between meals on bagels and cream cheese, corn chips, and pretty much any other fatty, salty junk he wanted, all provided by me, his loving, clueless mother.

After that embarrassing encounter with Rick, I went in the other direction: I made Zack "vegetable parfait" as an after-school snack, a tall glass layered with carrots, tomatoes, and celery. And though he actually did eat these concoctions, he also saw them as a delightful *amuse bouche* intended to whet his appetite for the rest of the afternoon's snacking.

When my friend Cale hears this, she tells me that if one of her kids asks for a snack, "I'll say, 'Tell me what you've had today.' That way we can fill in the gaps in their diet, they feel empowered because they have a choice, and they're learning how to care for their bodies." Of course this approach assumes she knows what her kids are supposed to be eating, and how much, and that her kids are amenable to working with her. And while this sounds all well and good, Andy and I can't help wondering if maybe Cale's kids are a little more adaptable or perhaps less defiant. Ultimately, though, this just makes us realize that if we didn't already know and love Cale, we might have to dislike her for being so clearheaded.

Five years after that telling day in Rick's office, while we're still not doing as well as Cale, a lot has changed for the better. Andy and I are now the parents of two; the four of us live with our fourteen-year-old mutt, Roxy, in a three-bedroom colonial with a picket fence. All the important family action happens in three rooms: the TV room, of course; the kitchen, natch; and the dining room. The latter is an autumnal burnt orange on the bottom and a soothing sunset yellow above. We eat family dinners on a table we bought at an auction nearly a decade ago; I still remember the thrill of raising my hand in the winning bid and the look of surprise on Andy's face as I did.

The table is actually a hundred-year-old door mounted on turned legs; it already looked beat up when we bought it, so we never have to worry about nicks, scratches or watermarks. We have six red cane chairs placed around it — they are starting to fall apart, but we don't want new ones because now they match the dining-room gestalt — so the table easily accommodated us when we became a family of four. I sit on one side, Andy and Zack sit on the other, and oddly, Maya is at the head. This started when she was still in a high chair and her legs wouldn't fit under the side of the table. Now, when we try to shake this configuration up, we all feel out of sorts. We can squeeze up to nine people around the table, but after that we have to send the kids in the other room to eat.

Though our setup looks pretty good from the street, all is not as it appears, because try as we might, there's still a lot we're doing wrong: the kids watch way too much TV, we yell at them too loudly and too often, and we hardly ever remember to have them brush their teeth in the mornings. (See eight fillings above.) There's room for improvement in so many areas it's hard to keep track.

Then, to top it all off, there's mealtime, which is basically a mess. Here's the story in a nutshell: The kids want to eat everything we don't want them to. They don't want to eat what we do want them to. Their likes and dislikes cancel each other's options out. The end.

Feeling slightly overwhelmed, we decide to write down everyone's food preferences so that before moving forward with an ambitious makeover, we can see where we stand now. Drum roll, please . . .

The Lists:
Zack won't eat (in alphabetical order):

Bananas
Cheese (including mac 'n' cheese, grilled cheese, or just
    plain cheese, with the glaring exception of fried cheese
    clumps and, since he turned seven, pizza)

Some vegetables (eggplant, squash)
Yogurt

Not bad, right? Zack's limitations are far outweighed by his adventurousness. He started at five with snails in black bean sauce and has never looked back. Bluefish, grilled sardines, tuna tartare, almost any fruit or vegetable — even raw milk. Despite his minor list of dislikes, he's a fabulous dining companion and he's great to cook for.

Then we get to Maya, who, at only five, can be somewhat excused for her pickiness. Unfortunately, it's easier to catalog what she does eat rather than what she doesn't. Basically, she gives the nod to:

Beans
Bread, crackers, and cereal (all made with white flour)
French fries
Fruit
Some meat, as long as it's salty (bacon, pan-fried slices of ham, the occasional burger)
Some vegetables some of the time (if the moon is in the right phase)
Soy nut butter (someone else gave her some last summer, and to my shock, she tossed peanut butter over for the stuff)

The biggest problem we have with Maya is that just because she liked something yesterday, or even an hour ago, doesn't mean she'll like it now or, possibly, ever again. For example, take cheese. It used to be a staple, until out of the blue she says she doesn't like it. That holds true until her best friend comes over to play and has cheese for a snack, after which Maya will eat it again but only the kind that her friend ate. And so on. What she'll eat becomes a daily riddle—until recently it was everything Zack hates, like cheese, bananas, yogurt—but today? Who knows. Maya is a living Zen koan: unfathomable, but at least she keeps us on our toes.

Finally we come to Andy, who makes the two kids look like extreme food connoisseurs.

Before I delight in trashing my husband, let me be clear: I adore the man. He's artistic and romantic and thoughtful and funny and warm. Oh, and patient. Endlessly patient. He's a great photographer. He brings me hot tea in bed sometimes. Plus, he's a fantastic cook. However, Andy is by far the pickiest eater, in the "adult" category, I've ever met. Does it seem like I'm being dramatic? You haven't tried feeding Andy.

When defending himself, my beleaguered husband tells me he has something called a "geographic tongue." He goes on to explain, citing no science to back his theory, that this kind of tongue affects his taste buds in such a way that he can't eat the following:

All condiments (including ketchup, mustard, and mayo)
Casseroles of any kind
Cheese, soft: cream, blue, ricotta, fresh mozzarella (he only
    used to eat American, but now he's branched out; these
    four are still verboten, though)
Cilantro
Dessert (except very occasionally)
Lots of seafood (clams, mussels, oysters, bluefish, etc.)
Many vegetables, too numerous to list
Most sauces (including barbecue, gravy, mustard, and
    cream)
Most stews (unless he's made them, and even then he'll care-
    fully pick out the meat and leave the wet parts behind)
Oatmeal

Pickles (unless he's made them)
Sour cream
Squash (winter, summer)
Tofu
Tomatoes in any form (fresh, dried, sauce, etc.)
Vinegar
Yogurt

I'm sure I'm forgetting something.
   And now, to be fair, I'll list my own food restrictions:

Basil, carrots, cherries, and peas, raw (love all four, but they
   make me either break out in hives or experience varying
   degrees of throat closure; strangely, I can eat them all
   either dried or cooked)
Skate (makes my lips itchy, which is so weird, but then
   Zack had it one night and the same thing happened to
   him, so at least there are two of us)
Cilantro (loathe it)

CALL IN THE CAVALRY

In other words, we're at a standstill. Before we can go any further,
we're going to need help from a pro. No one will be able to change
our children's or my husband's dietary preferences, although come
to think of it, maybe we should look for a hypnotist? No, we're not
quite desperate enough to go that route — at least not yet; instead,
we're just hoping to find an expert who can evaluate our family
diet and give us specific feedback on what we're doing right and
wrong so we can improve on it.
   We've arrived at step 1 of our meal makeover: consult a nutritionist.

I do a quick Web search and find someone who has all sorts of impressive letters after her name; plus, she works at a children's nutrition research center. I couldn't have found a more perfect match.

I call her up, and after an awkward five-minute conversation, she tersely tells me she doesn't want to work with me. I'm horrified. *Why not?* Well, she tells me, she can't help, because "organic isn't a sustainable message. If some people want to pay more for organic food," she goes on testily, "that's *fine,* but we already have enough trouble getting people to make healthy choices from regular grocery stores." This nutritionist doesn't think it makes any difference whether or not people eat organic because "our food supply is safe." You could push me over with a feather I'm so surprised. Organic food controversial? Who knew?

Actually, I did; I just didn't realize that her research center is partnered with the USDA. As in the same USDA that set off a firestorm in 1997 when it released its first proposed set of organic standards saying that farms could be certified as organic even if they used genetic modification and sewage sludge in food. After receiving more than 275,000 complaints from the public, the agency agreed to revise the rules to exclude all of this in foods to be labeled USDA-certified organic.

In other words, this nutritionist who doesn't think organics are a sustainable message works alongside the same USDA that tried to dumb down organic standards back in the 1990s. She also informs me that we'll have a hard time finding a nutritionist who supports organic foods. (She sounds a little *angry* when she tells me this, right before abruptly ending the conversation. Maybe a little too much sewage sludge in her diet?) I'm hoping she's wrong, but what if she's not? I'm a little worried.

Well, if we can't find a nutritionist, we'll just have to wing it and go by the books. There's just too much tomfoolery in food these days, and we need to figure it out. Take organic food, for example. While basic standards were salvaged thanks to public outcry, some believe that the USDA has turned "certified organic" into a bad joke.

We'd say we don't know what they're talking about, except that the Organic Trade Association, in a report on "the past, present and future of the organic food industry," writes that by 2025, "anything and everything could have an organic version," including "organic Twinkies™, pets and edible packaging."

Not knowing where else to turn, and kind of depressed at the thought of organic pets (they must mean pet food, right?), I call our pediatrician, Rick, who tells me about a book by Susan Roberts, PhD.

Dr. Roberts is both a professor of nutrition and a professor of psychiatry at Tufts University. Her doctorate is from the University of Cambridge. She is also, Rick tells me, the coauthor of *Feeding Your Child for Lifelong Health*. Rick says that the book is "very interesting," which I hear as understated doctor-talk for "extremely excellent," so I immediately buy a copy.

Still feeling slightly off-kilter after my encounter with the angry nutritionist, I nervously contact Dr. Roberts. Fortunately, she is willing to work with us after all. We decide to keep a weeklong family food diary, which, once we're done, we'll send off for her perusal.

Keep a Food Diary

One kid can be the record keeper; another can be the artist. At the end of one week, have a family meeting to see what you're all doing right and where you could stand to make some changes.

Day 1:
I can't help noticing, now that we're really paying attention, just how much nutrient- and fiber-free white flour we eat around here; just as I'm mulling this over, Andy shows up with a baguette to serve with our pasta dinner.

"We need to eat less white flour, babe," I say.

He doesn't reply.

Meanwhile, Zack is being *so* helpful and cooperative. He comes into my office to ask for a notebook so he can start keeping our all-family food diary; he writes everyone's breakfasts down in the neatest print ever. Maybe he doesn't understand where I'm going with all this?

Day 2:
More of the same from Zack. He even tells us about the ice cream he had at school. If we weren't keeping track of our food this week, we'd never have known. We later learn that the kids' days were filled with Goldfish crackers, pizza, pasta, and soda, although there were also apples, grapes, and a salad for Zack.

Speaking of Zack, he watches over my shoulder as I write down my own entry: granola, vegetable soup, squash, and broccolini with pasta. To him, my day looks practically perfect. When he leaves the room, I whisper to Andy, "I also had an éclair!"

"I know," he evenly replies, the Switzerland of the family.

I shake my head in disgust at myself and then, once I've made sure Zack has left the room, write it down. Maybe I'm a bad person, a liar, a deceiver, but as I told my friend Sheila while we were waiting for our kindergartners to come out of school one afternoon, sometimes it seems that an éclair is all I can claim as mine. Forget about a room of my own. I'm just gunning for a pastry.

Night of Day 2:
About the bottle of wine Andy and I shared at dinner . . .

I love beer and wine, but I usually stick to one or two glasses. Three is over my limit. By the end of the meal I look over at my husband with a big grin on my face and announce, "I'm drunk!"

He's not sorry to hear it.

Morning of Day 3:
"Zackie's getting tired of this food diary," Maya tells me. Who isn't? I'm ready to hang it up too. It's just more proof that I'm not on top of things around here. Who needs it?

Day 4:
Our friends Bob and Mary Jo have closed their restaurant for their annual art fair and have covered the bar with snacks for the customers. "Help yourself," Bob generously says to the kids, which they do. Lunch is candy and cookies, with a few chips thrown in for good measure. I pretend not to see, but later I remember we have to quiz them so we can write it down and show it to the noted nutritionist.

Day 5, Morning:
Or is that mourning? I'm in my home office when I hear our crazy but lovable mutt, Roxy, making a funny noise in the other room. I go in to check on her and she's shaking, having trouble standing up, and her face is twitching. She's had a stroke; she has a fifty-fifty chance of making it. The household has been turned upside down.

Day 6:
School lets out at 11 a.m. three days this week, our beloved dog is on a deathwatch, and the kids are a wreck (as are Andy and I) — so for a treat, I take the kids out to a Japanese restaurant for

lunch. While we're eating, Maya asks what "put to sleep" really *means*. Moments later, both kids are crying and I'm casually waving the server over with a fake smile on, trying to get the bill.

Day 7:
None of us is doing well with the possibility of losing Roxy, and all we can focus on is getting her to eat, because if she doesn't, she'll be gone within a day. We sauté up some hamburger, cut up a chicken breast, and offer her wet dog food, which she's never had. She either won't eat or she can't. Then Zack, in a moment of inspiration, brings over a small dish of plain yogurt and places it right under her nose: she takes a few small licks. By the end of the day, she's graduated to hamburger.

I'm ready to give up on our food diary, but when I suggest this to the kids they cry out in protest. I still don't think they quite understand what's going to come of all this, but they obviously want to see the project through to the end of the week. So we keep it for another day — the one the kids spend with their surrogate grandma and Andy's office manager, Sue, who loves to spoil them; hence, for the last entry, which they could have avoided recording if they'd played their cards right, Zack writes down chips, cookies, candy. Andy says he's going to have a talk with Sue.

The upshot of the week is that Maya has had either pasta or baguette for dinner five nights out of the seven, although one night she had a variation on the theme in the form of a baked potato. Her mornings and days were filled with Cheerios, crackers, and pancakes, with a banana, apple, or grapes thrown in here and there, thanks to pressure from me.

Zack's week looks better, but there are still some areas of concern. On the upside, he's had crab cakes, coq au vin, salads, and falafel and snacks of rice cakes, all sorts of fruit, and raw vegetables. But his week was also full of white pasta, lots of pizza, and far more snacks during the day than I provided (or knew about).

My diet looks pretty good — in my diary I have Arctic char, though it's in a butter sauce, but there's also coq au vin, falafel, crab cakes, and lentils with sausage. There's baguette and white potato written down a couple too many times, and fatty stuffing because I was craving it; all in all, it's neither terrible nor great. As for Andy, he's recently stopped buying muffins and chips for lunch, and now he's eating some dry cereal along with his morning coffee, both of which are a big improvement for him. He's had chicken and crab cakes and falafel along with Zack and me; during the days he went for bagels and one or two doughnuts but also edamame, carrots, and avocado sushi. Like me, his diet could be better, but it could also be a lot worse.

I send the record off to Dr. Roberts and anxiously await her reply. A couple days later, I get a note back: "OK, so a few things here . . . You and Andy eat better than your kids: lentils, raisin bran, etc. Why aren't they eating what you eat??"

She's kidding, right? Yanking my chain? It's all I dream of, Maya eating what we eat, Zack just saying no to soda. I consider the fact that our diet is even this good no less than a *miracle*. This is killing me.

She goes on: "I can see some specific things with the kids' diets — lots of juice, white bread (for everyone. There's good whole wheat bread you could substitute for baguette . . .), and I suspect you have at least 10 snacks in the house (Cheez-Its, chips, corn chips, Oreos), but only three kinds of fruit (I saw apples, grapes, and kiwi only). The variety ratio needs to be improved so that fruit gets more interesting and snacks get less interesting."

I reply: "As for the kids eating ice cream, cupcakes, chocolate Teddy Grahams, Cheez-Its — we have NONE of these in the house.

This all happens when they're at school. Zack actually asked some girl in his class for money so he could buy ice cream one day, and I don't think he ever paid her back, which is another issue. My kids are not above begging money and snacks from other kids. What's a mother to do?"

She sympathizes but offers no fast and easy answers, which is what I'm hoping for.

"That said," she continues, "you are also doing great in important ways."

All right!

"I love Brussels sprouts and so do my family, but yours is the FIRST dietary record I have seen where other kids eat them also!"

That would be Zack, not Maya, but still. Ha.

"And don't worry about good fat. Peanut butter" — although she must not have seen that it's actually soy nut butter — "oil in cooking, olive oil for dipping with whole wheat bread as a snack, all fine stuff. And cholesterol that comes with other goodies (like eggs) is fine also. It is butter and cream that aren't good."

This is pretty good news, except for the last part about butter and cream, which, honestly, we might have to ignore for the moment. There's already so much to take in. Then she hits me with this: "They are probably not getting enough iron. You might have a hemoglobin check, or consider multivitamins."

She tells me that *one in seven* kids in Massachusetts is iron deficient, and that "iron in particular has permanent effects on development. If you don't get enough in early childhood, you get deficient and it has cognitive effects that are probably not reversible, or at least, not totally. And make sure it doesn't happen when they're teens also."

Okay, we get it. They need iron. Where do we get it? Dr. Roberts tells me that some of the best sources are red meat and eggs. Of course, many people, including us, are eating much less meat and eggs than in years past. Also, lots of junky, sugary cereals and processed foods are iron fortified, so those of us who aren't eating bad cereals and mass-produced sliced bread are missing out. In other words, if we actually were able to follow a vegetable and fruit-rich, low-meat, low-processed-foods diet, it could very well hurt our children, although, come to think of it, maybe they could get their vitamins and iron from the fortified snacks they mooch off their friends.

Curious about where we stand on vitamin-enriched processed foods, Andy and I go into our cupboard to check labels; the Cheerios have iron in them, but otherwise? Nothing in the house has more than 4 percent of the recommended daily allowances. I do a little Web surfing and find out that the symptoms of iron deficiency include fatigue (check for both kids), pale skin (we are in the beginning of one of New England's legendary five month winters, but check for both kids), and irritability (check for both kids, in spades). With fingers crossed that neither of the kids has suffered irreversible brain damage yet, we inform them that they must start taking a multivitamin with iron, stat. ("But we don't want to make them stronger," Andy jokes after one particularly tough morning.)

Naturally, just to make life more complex, getting too much iron can be just as harmful as getting too little. In her book, Dr. Roberts writes, "It is almost impossible to get too much iron from regular foods . . . Supplements, however, are a different story. Children's multivitamins are considered safe, and indeed recommended. But supplements containing only iron *should never be given to children* unless prescribed by their pediatrician for a specific problem."

She goes on to explain, "Surveys have reported that more than 50 percent of children in the United States consume inadequate amounts of one or more of three crucial minerals [iron, calcium, and zinc]. This is one of the major public health problems of our time. Virtually all children are at risk, both affluent and poor alike . . . Even mild shortages of these essential three can have serious long-term health consequences."

One of the major public health problems of our time, she said. This book was published in 1999, so I ask her if this still holds true today; she says it does. Come to think of it, the kids are probably lacking calcium too.

After this exchange, we take a few days off to catch our breath. I thought maybe she'd tell us to stop fighting about white flour so much, which she did, or that maybe the kids were begging too much sugar from friends at school, which she also did, but we never expected anything like this; it's terrible news, and totally unexpected.

Really, I tell Andy, we should call Rick and schedule a blood test for the kids so we can get to the bottom of this. He strongly disagrees, perhaps sensing, as I have yet to, the children's growing concern over the direction family dinners are heading. I'm not sure when they got clued in — maybe it's through osmosis, or maybe I've unthinkingly been nagging them more than usual — but unlike when we were keeping our food diary, now they seem to understand that we're headed in a new, healthier direction, and anxiety levels have risen commensurately. Therefore, Andy doesn't feel that making them get stuck with needles in the name of our monster meal makeover would be such a good idea, so for the kids: no bloodletting, but multivitamins. And calcium.

I still have a decade's worth of questions about kids' nutrition.

Supplements

Supplements are a fifteen-billion-dollar industry,
according to the National Academy of Sciences.
Everyone wants a piece of the action, so buy
multivitamins from a company that's been in business
for a while. Look for bottles that have at least ten
vitamins and minerals listed. Some people claim that
bee pollen is nature's own multivitamin, but it's also
highly allergenic.

Fortunately, I still have Dr. Roberts on the line, and so, confusing as it is, and putting my shock about the iron thing aside, I soldier on. "What about the contention that the calcium in dairy isn't easily absorbed?" I ask. "Are calcium supplements better than / worse than / equal to calcium-added OJ?"

What I don't ask is, How much calcium do we even need? Some people say that while Americans have the highest dairy intake in the world, we also have the highest rates of osteoporosis. Some say that when the source of calcium is not dairy but rather soy, bone density is better. However, considering that our kids like milk, and considering that my husband and son hate tofu, and considering that three of us don't just like cheese, we *love* it, I may have to give up on this one.

Dr. Roberts replies that calcium is absorbed fine from dairy, and that among the supplements, calcium citrate has a slightly better absorption than calcium carbonate, but that they all work pretty well.

Despite the multivitamin hullabaloo, Dr. Roberts writes, "It's important for children to obtain most of their essential nutrients from foods, rather than relying on supplements . . . While the classic vitamins have been known for decades, there are many other substances in foods that have important effects on health." Shoot, just when we thought we could give in and feed the kids vitamin- and iron-fortified Sugar Smacks three times a day.

Okay, okay: food still matters. Wondering about food-based sources of the good stuff, I come across a vegetarian, calcium-rich sample menu that looks like this:

Breakfast
2 slices whole grain bread with almond butter
1 medium orange

Lunch
1 whole wheat pita with black bean hummus
Kale salad with tahini dressing

Snack
Whole grain muffin with blackstrap molasses

Dinner
Tofu (extra firm with calcium), bok choy, broccoli, and
    almonds stir-fry
Brown rice

Snack
Tofu cheese and whole wheat crackers
3 figs

I wonder what the kids would say if we offered them kale salad with tahini dressing for lunch. That would go over well in the school cafeteria. In our house, brown rice and whole grain breads remain sources not of nutrition but of contention. And tofu cheese for a snack?

And so, faced with unrealistic alternatives along with a family who loves meat and dairy, from now on, since our children show no obvious adverse effects to it, I choose to believe that dairy is fine — and, in fact, as Andy always says, everything in moderation is fine. But, hedging my bets, I also add almonds, figs, and kale to the shopping list. Healthy foods are worth a try, even though often no one but me likes them. It's true that waste happens when I get ambitious like this, but I can't help myself.

And then we finally get back to reading over the professor's reasonable daily dietary recommendations: "a cup each of fruits and veggies, 2 cups milk or yogurt, a serving or two of meat/eggs/fish/beans, a couple of slices of bread, spreads or fillings of any kind to serve with the bread and you're about there." Wait a minute, spreads or fillings *of any kind*? We definitely won't tell the kids she said this, because they'd obviously come back at us suggesting the likes of Nutella and Fluff.

Then, she adds, we can also offer "a couple of treats in small servings — say, ¼ cup ice milk." If we served Zack and Maya ¼ cup of ice milk for dessert, they'd torment us about it for the next decade. After mulling it over for a few hours, though, I add ice milk to the grocery list. I'm frighteningly suggestible.

For snacks, she suggests bread and nut butter; ham sandwich; carrots with hummus; cereal and milk; nuts and raisins; celery sticks with light cream cheese; yogurt with or without fruit (or mixed half and half to cut the sugar), with or without granola.

I went from offering snacks of corn chips, which make kids pudgy, to only providing fruits and veggies, which left them hungry.

Now there's a happy middle ground to pursue. Why didn't I think of this?

Realizing she's answered most of my questions about the kids, I decide to ask about adult nutrition; after all, we matter, if only because without us our kids would have no one to fetch their snacks. Dr. Roberts had already told me that "iron, zinc, etc., are much less of a worry for adults — because you eat more total food, it is easier to get enough and requirements are smaller proportional to calories." But she still recommends a multivitamin with iron for moms, and a multivitamin without iron for dads.

Unfortunately, there are no food-based vitamins plus iron that the kids find palatable, so every morning they end up gagging dramatically and making a big scene out of asking for water to wash the bitter pill down; the good news is, this means they won't want to sneak any while we're not looking. Not that either of them would, but their old iron-free vitamins tasted like candy, so understandably they got confused.

I also cross my fingers in the hope that Zack doesn't discover red meat is a good source of iron because it's all he wants to eat and everyone, including Dr. Roberts, says we shouldn't have too much of it. We'll continue pouring a glass or two of calcium-added OJ and also give the kids calcium supplements, because they're not getting enough of that either. And we'll stay on course with our whole-foods-based diet, never letting on that Lucky Charms and Frosted Flakes are chock full of vitamins and iron.

When I roughly fill Andy in on what Dr. Roberts has said, he exclaims, "We eat better than almost anyone else in America!" He's not the only one who thought we were doing pretty well.

("Mom," Zack calls up the stairs on the fourth morning of our new regime, "do I have to take these vitamins?"

"Yes," I call back.

Maya comes over to tell me, "He just whispered 'Damn it' under his breath."

"It's not me telling him he has to take them," I calmly explain to my still loyal five-year-old. "It's the nutritionist."

Maya yells down the stairs, "Zack, the nutritionist is making you take the vitamins."

"No," he yells back. "Mom is.")

Just when I think I've gotten the matter under control, a friend points out that we use cast-iron pans. Ah hell, I'd forgotten about that. Does it matter? "They do leach iron," Dr. Roberts tells me cheerily. "It's a good thing to think about!"

That's when I wonder if Dr. Roberts would be willing to take over the feeding of my two young. And my one not-so-young.

Chapter 1 ½

. . . .

At the Table: Take 1

The four of us are sitting at the table, forks at the ready. As usual, Maya's at the head, I'm on one side, Andy and Zack are on the other. This is all good, because researchers say that kids who have dinner with their families most nights are less likely to abuse alcohol and drugs or exhibit symptoms of stress. They're also supposedly more likely to get better grades and eat more healthfully. But what do the researchers say when no one can agree on what to eat, and then this lack of a shared vision actually causes rather than reduces family strife? What then?

On tonight's menu: "natural" pork loin that's been pan-seared, then finished off in the oven and topped with crispy pan-fried mushrooms; maple-and-butter-glazed carrots; organic broccoli; organic baked potato; and a baguette from a local bakery.

This meal seems relatively healthy. Because this is pork loin, and not chops or ribs, the meat is a low-fat source of protein; there are two types of colorful vegetables plus mushrooms; and while in an ideal world we'd have used sweet potatoes instead of russets, and whole wheat instead of white, I think even Dr. Roberts would give this menu a nod of approval. But something about it rubs me the wrong way. It just seems so *American*. Literally, meat and potatoes. And boring, ubiquitous broccoli.

This doesn't bother Zack or Andy in the least; they're both happily digging into everything. I'm eating with gusto too, except for the pork loin, which I'm realizing I don't like as much as I used to. It's kind of chalky; you might even call it flavorless. As for Maya, she has allowed only bread, skinless potato balls mashed with milk and butter, one small piece of broccoli and a few carrot coins onto her plate.

"Why don't you try the broccoli?" I ask. "It's really good tonight." She's not biting, so I add, "It's salty. And yours looks like *baby broccoli*!" I'm not too proud to make a vegetable sound cute if it will pique Maya's interest, and this time that's just what it does. She gives me a suspicious look, but she also picks up the lone floret on her plate and takes the tiniest nibble possible.

"Do you like it?" I press.

"Not really," she says, delicately placing the rest of it back on her plate.

Neither Andy nor I want to get into bribes or trades or threats with Maya — take one bite and in return we'll give you sugar or fat or money, or if you don't take a bite you can't have dessert or TV or love — so I drop it. Still, she's only gained two pounds in the last year, and not even one ounce of that weight has come from anything green. But while we won't bribe or threaten her, we will encourage and entice her, which is exactly what Andy does a few minutes later.

"I think you'd like these carrots, My."

"A *chef* gave me the recipe," I add, trying to make them sound exciting. "They're sweet." She picks one up between her finger and thumb and takes a taste.

"Yum, they're good!" she exclaims. I smile, though not too broadly. I'm well aware that if at all possible it's best to keep a poker face during mealtimes, even if your insides are churning with frustration, or jumping with glee. "That chef who teached you this recipe is a good cook!" she goes on. "But even though I like them, I don't want you to give them to me for dinner ever again."

I smile again, this time a little more tightly. Andy looks across the table at me sympathetically. Okay, point taken. She's done with carrots and broccoli for the night. But regardless of what she wants, we will keep making and serving vegetables, flavoring them with salt and maple syrup as needed, because the day will come that she'll take another bite. Of that we're sure. At least, we have our fingers crossed.

Chapter 2

. . . .

Holiday Hurdle

FAMILY DINNERS

Andy calls home on his cell phone at lunchtime. As usual, he's on the road for his job as a real estate appraiser, looking at houses in various towns all over eastern Mass. Also as usual, I'm intensely focused on the computer screen in our home office, which has a glass door and is adjacent to the dining room, placing me well within the reach of curious eyes and ears at all times.

"Just checking in," Andy says, and then adds, "Any thoughts on dinner?"

It's an apt question because it only recently occurred to me that in our enthusiasm to get going on this meal makeover, we jumped straight into the heart of vitamins and minerals without taking even a moment to consider the bigger picture. We already know family dinners are supposed to be good for kids' overall well-being. But we're surprised when we read in *Family Mealtime as a Context of Development and Socialization,* a collection of scholarly essays published last year, that there's research showing that family mealtimes "may provide richer opportunities for vocabulary development than . . . reading books with children."

Back in the days when Andy and I were what he refers to as "single," meaning married but childless, we'd start talking about the next night's dinner nearly twenty-four hours in advance. Planning, shopping for, cooking, and eating a meal together at the end of each day was like an exclamation point. Now, though, dinner is more like an ellipsis, because while we want to plan out our meals for the week, and we want to try healthy, new recipes, and we want dinnertime to increase the kids' vocabulary, the reality's a lot more . . . I don't know . . . real world. That is to say, disappointing.

The iconic American family dinner — the sort that Andy remembers from his own childhood, when his mom dished up a square meal for her family of four every night at six — dates back to the mid-nineteenth century. "As standardized schedules of school and work began to impress their rhythms on middle-class family life," writes Simone Cinotto in *Family Mealtime,* "there had emerged a carefully ordered progression of breakfast, lunch and dinner, which 'marked off the middle class from the big lunch eaters down the social scale.'" The mid-1800s was also when cookbooks, guides, and handbooks on domestic life began to appear, such as *The American Woman's Home, or Principles of Domestic Science.*

Around this time is when a separate room devoted solely to mealtimes — the dining room — came into being. Of course, three meals a day and a room set aside just for eating was only feasible for the middle class; others weren't so lucky. The "vast majority of freed women (former slaves) continued to work outside the home for long hours," making family dinners impossible. And "until the World War I years, many poorer urban white workers were also unable to adopt the middle-class model of family mealtimes."

In other words, given the historical context, family dinners were really a luxury. Not only do they presuppose that there's enough food, but also the time and space for all family members to sit together and eat it. Indeed, "the Victorian family meal saw its widespread realization in the United States only during the postwar 1950s, when prosperity permitted the majority of the population to join the middle class." But hasn't the family dinner gone the way of the eight-track tape? Not according to *Family Mealtime,* which reports that the 2003 National Survey of Children's Health showed that 80 percent of families with children ages six to eleven eat together four or more times a week. Apparently the demise of the family dinner has been vastly overreported.

Eating together isn't a goal in all societies, however. "In China, for example, older-generation family members take food before the younger generation." And in Samoa, "older children are expected to help young adults to prepare and serve meals." Other cultures may be onto something here.

In the book, Elinor Ochs and Merav Shohet note that in a recent study "Italian family dinners did not include a dessert, and Italian parents did not use sweets to cajole children to eat." Now there's something to think about. Andy and I recently instituted a policy of sweet desserts on weekends only; on weeknights, we have fruit after dinner. This rule does seem to have lessened the fights and negotiations about sugar — "What can I have?" "How much can I have?" "He has more than I do," and so on — at least during the week. But now it's also clear that by having fruit for dessert, we're emulating a European sensibility, which makes it that much more exciting.

Ochs and Shohet also note that in the same study cited above, Italians used "a rich grammar of positive affect to praise both the food and the person who prepared or purchased it." So when ask-

ing for more meat, one young Italian child said what amounted
to, "Mama, this appealing, nice, little, delicate piece, I want it."
Why can't Zack and Maya sound this captivating when they're
asking for seconds?

AND SO, WHEN Andy calls on his cell asking if I've thought about
dinner, the answer is yes, a lot. But I automatically say no, because what I'm really dreaming of right then — vegetarian chili, a
long-simmered tomato sauce, Persian eggplant with pomegranate
juice and marjoram — can't happen owing to Andy's food foibles.
I know from past experience that if I start pining over meals that
cannot be, I'll get mad. Then Andy says he's about to pass a grocery store; he'll stop in and see what looks good.

Soon afterward, when I'm once again engrossed in research for
an article, he comes through the front door with a bag of grocer-
ies. Today he even has lunch for me — a salad with beets, eggplant,
and tofu to prove he supports my gustatory preferences even if he
will never share them.

I take a break to help unload the chicken and potatoes he's
bought for roasting, along with broccoli and a baguette, and then
he's off to his office, which is about a three-minute drive away. Five
hours later, he comes home and heads straight into the kitchen to
cook a sort of boring, still eminently American dinner for four
(meat, veg, carbs), and I head back to the computer after being
with Zack and Maya all afternoon.

The husband as the family's primary food gatherer and cook
is not typical, it's true; even 150 years into family dinners, more
often than not it's usually the woman who covers these bases.
But given our circumstances — two wildly fussy eaters and one
ten-year-old boy, a mom who works from home catch-as-catch-

can and a dad who's on the road every day — this arrangement works for all of us, although the fact that I have to clean up after dinner most nights is still up for discussion. Who wouldn't rather be the cook? But when I do make a meal, it often just flames the fire of resentment that I can't make something with tomatoes.

I know how spoiled this sounds — pretty much all my friends say they're jealous of me for having married such a talented and willing chef — but when I remind them what Andy won't eat, they back down and nod their heads in understanding. They also don't invite us over for dinner very often; Cale says she's actually scared to cook for Andy. With good reason.

SETBACK I: FRIED

Days later, I'm still haunted by the thought of that Italian child asking for another "appealing, nice, little, delicate" piece of meat. In our house no one is even close to this charming, and now we're going ahead and making things worse. Indeed, we've only just begun this quest for a better diet and it's already starting to feel like one of those "clean the closets" days; at first, it's exciting as you pull out the swim goggles you thought you lost two years ago. Soon enough, though, you realize there's far more crap in here than you ever could have imagined, but it's too late to stop now because the stuff is already strewn all over the house. The only way out is through. Nothing enchanting about it.

When we first embarked on this makeover, things were mapped out so neatly. We had a perfect plan: we were going to take the kids to meet farmers, nutritionists, and fishermen, all in an effort to educate them about food and make them more like delightful Italian children. But now? No one wants to do anything if it's even remotely related to health and planetary wellness.

To make things worse, the holidays are almost here. Even I know I can't deny the kids treats between Halloween and New Year's unless I want a full-blown mutiny on my hands. But the truth is, though the only change we've instituted so far has been getting the kids to take vitamins — or trying to anyway — that's already been enough to get their hackles up.

Now, any time I counter a request for potato chips or cookies with the suggestion of squash soup or a salad, Zack sneers and says something cutting like, "Oh c'mon, Mom, give us a break. You think a few potato chips are going to kill us?" But at least then he'll help himself to some carrots and cherry tomatoes before stomping out of the room. Meanwhile, Maya's not nearly as amenable to vegetables as Zack is, so she's more likely to just start wailing. As for easygoing Andy, I can see the frustration in his eyes when he thinks I'm making life harder for everyone with my so-called high standards.

Suddenly, I'm glad it's almost Hanukkah and New Year's, because I have a plan. Based on everyone's opposition toward me and my big ideas right now, I accept that I must win back some hearts and minds, even if it takes a little sugar and spice to do so. The holidays are as good a justification as any.

As the one who sets an example for his sister and the one who feels the most deprived lately, Zack is the most important one to win over first. In fact, things between us have gotten so bad that I'm thinking of offering him a fryer. I know he wants one because Andy got me one for Hanukkah three years ago, and when I had taken one look at it and then shoved the box away with my foot, Zack was totally bummed out.

"Aren't you going to open it?" Andy asked hopefully.

"Open it? I'm not even going to touch it. You have to return it."

Both his and Zack's faces fell. "Are you sure? Just think of everything we could make . . ."

Oh, I was thinking, all right. Thinking about the soft, warm doughnuts and salty potatoes (both fries and chips), the tender calamari and clams, but most of all, the crispy, juicy fried chicken. I could well imagine what we could do if we had a fryer, which is exactly why I said we couldn't keep it.

And so it shows just how low I've sunk that a mere three years later I offer one to Zack. He accepts.

Does it seem like I'm giving the kids mixed messages by saying no to fried food and then suddenly changing my mind and buying them a fryer? Guilty as charged. Consistency is the bedrock of good parenting, but knowing it and following through on it are two entirely different things.

Anyway, it's much easier to give in on the fryer because we are only days away from the start of Hanukkah, the festival of fried foods (that is, lights), which means we have culture, religion, and history to fall back on as some of the best excuses around. At least for a week. After that? I'm hoping everyone will get sick of it, or forget about it, or that it will be quietly relegated to the basement, like the cappuccino maker Andy and I bought ourselves as a wedding present almost fifteen years ago.

On day 1 of our all-family fried food binge, Andy decides to make beignets with a chili-spiked dark chocolate sauce. "I don't think the kids are going to like these," I tell him. He mumbles something incomprehensible and makes them anyway. They're a marvel — soft inside, crisp outside, dipped into that rich, bittersweet, spicy warm chocolate — but I was right about the kids. "They're not sweet enough," Maya complains. Aw, too bad.

Day 2: latkes, which aren't as good as usual because there's no pan to flatten them against, so they turn out more like latke balls. "Mine are better," a friend who's come over for lunch with her family blurts out. Later, Andy and I laugh at her uncharacteristic honesty, but we can see where latkes would bring that out in a person. Next: Zack and his friend Andrew, who's never been to our house before, decide to make potato chips. I tell Andrew's mom, Holly, about the project, mostly because Andrew is going to be returning home with some leftovers. She comments sarcastically, "That's a healthy snack." She probably thinks homemade potato chips are the norm here.

That night, as we're talking about our new life with the fryer, Andy asks, "What else can we fry? Onion strings? Mmm! Or what happens if you put a whole ear of corn in?"

"Are you going to fry an ear of corn?" I ask incredulously.

"I dunno. These are the things a man wonders about," he answers philosophically before adding, "We haven't made french fries yet. Fish and chips. Tempura! What would happen if you fried *fruit*?"

For a week solid, the house smells like a fast-food joint. The fried food train is still barreling full steam ahead. On the menu the night *after* Hanukkah: southern fried chicken, fluffy homemade biscuits, and baked yams. I admit that this is the chicken of my dreams, with a salty, shatteringly crisp skin and tender, juicy flesh; the biscuits are soft, pillowy, and fragrant from buttermilk. Still, I can't help feeling that we're going in the wrong direction. Weren't we going to improve our diet, not just make it more enjoyable?

SETBACK 2: BAKED

Just as I'm trying to figure out what to do for Maya, she interrupts my thoughts. "Daddy told me I can have a peanut butter and Fluff sandwich for lunch tomorrow." Unfortunately, we do have some "natural marshmallow crème" in the house but only because I needed it for an article I wrote. I look at Andy questioningly.

"I didn't commit," he says defensively. "I said she might not be able to."

That is, if I say no.

Zack sees my darkening face and quickly interjects, "Remember, you're Fun Mom."

Okay, fine, I'm Fun Mom, but still, I didn't agree to marshmallow sandwiches for lunch. This will not do; after all, we're going for containment here. The holidays offer the perfect cover for the fryer, because once they're over so is the makeover detour. Fluff sandwiches would set a dangerous precedent; we'd be living with the consequences for many school lunches to come. I ax the idea right away, but before Maya can start in I quickly add, "Do you want to make the train cake?" For weeks, she has been coveting a charming train cake pan she saw on a catalog cover.

She sucks in her breath and asks, "Really?"

"Really!" I answer, happy to get past the sticky sandwich problem. (Note to self: throw out Fluff.)

She claps her sweet little hands. "Mama, thank you thank you! I'm so happy! I'm so lucky! My mommy's the *best* mommy." Then, wanting to squeeze every last drop of goodwill possible from this healthy food hindrance, I ask if everyone wants to have a New Year's Day party, "and for dessert we could serve the train cakes!" After I say this I glance over at Andy. My eyes say, Sorry for not checking with you first, but apparently I got carried away. Or at

Dangerous Precedents

. . . .

Avoid setting dangerous precedents, like making an exception in the lunch box and giving in on that Fluff sandwich. Pretty soon, it will become expected. If you do make an exception, like doling out chocolate on a fruit dessert night, make sure everyone understands that this won't be happening every night. Scowl a little to drive the point home.

least I hope that's what my eyes say. Anyway, since I'm already in too deep to back out, I add that each kid will get to embellish his or her own car as an edible craft. "Could we buy candy to decorate it with, like in the picture?" Maya asks. "Of course we can," I answer expansively. She literally jumps up and down. I'm glad she's happy; then again, should she really be this happy about cake?

The Saturday after we get the pan, I'm exhausted and achy, plus my stomach hurts. In other words, it's a pretty typical day. Zack is upstairs playing with a friend, Maya is watching TV, and Andy is off doing something with tools in the basement. I'm just getting comfortable on the couch when, unbelievably, inconceivably, Maya appears in front of me and asks in a small voice, "Can we make the train cake now?"

In an effort to hide my horror and buy some time to think, I don't answer right away. "Well?" she says, now a touch impatiently, and in a last-ditch effort to salvage the moment for myself I ask, "Did you turn off the TV?" To my credit, my tone is neutral even though I'm aghast, thinking, Turn it back on!

She nods. "It was boring. Can we make the cake now?" she repeats.

How to Get Through the Holidays

1. Eat at home before a party, or load everyone up on even healthier snacks than usual.
2. Negotiate, bargain, and beg as needed. Let kids know they have to eat better during the rest of the day if there's a party. If there are two parties in one day (the horror), lay down rules before the festivities begin. (You can have two desserts, but you have to have healthy meals first; you can only have one dessert, but you can eat fewer vegetables—whatever occurs to you.)
3. Remember, the parties won't last forever.

All week I've been telling her that when Zack's friend is here on Saturday morning, the two of us will make the cake and that we'll freeze it until the day of the party. That moment has arrived. And so, without another second's hesitation, I answer brightly, "Of course we can!" As we're getting ready to fill the pans a few minutes later, though, it dawns on me that the train cars we're making aren't going to turn out quite as well as the ones on the magazine cover. Then again, the catalog probably had a whole kitchen staff turning out fifty pans of train cars until they got just the right ones for their all-day photo shoot. I'm morphing into Angry Baking Mom until Maya leans into me for a hug and says, "This is fun! We're a good team."

Considering we're in the middle of a makeover stumbling block, things could be worse.

Soon enough, the train cake New Year's Day party is upon us; it is an unmitigated success. After our friends leave, I pull Maya onto my lap. We're sitting in the living room in front of the fireplace; the fire is dying down. "Did you have fun?" I whisper in her ear, happily (and smugly) anticipating the warm moment we're about to share.

"Not really," she says, her lip curled up in a frown. "It wasn't what I expected."

It never is, I want to respond, but I hold my tongue.

"And," she adds, "I'm not even having fun right now, this minute." Then she looks straight in my eyes to drive the point home. Ruth's daughter Abby couldn't come tonight because she was sick, and so Maya, as the youngest kid at the party, had felt left out. I'm kind of happy to see that even for my sugar-loving little girl, a train cake is beside the point if you don't have a friend to share it with.

OUTNUMBERED

Right in the middle of all this baking and frying, I discover I'm up against forces far greater than I realized, not just in the house but in the world. Underminers are everywhere. This fear is confirmed when a mom I've met at Maya's swim class comes into the health club with a "goodie bag" for my family. Paige is a gorgeous, blond southern belle; she is, as she puts it, "a Versace girl in an L.L. Bean world."

After spending many Tuesday afternoons together, Paige knows all about my healthy ways, so she's brought my kids a pity offering of Moon Pies and GooGoo Clusters, sweet treats straight from the South brimming with sugar and trans fats. Paige, you shouldn't have! I want to say. Instead, I tell her what my kids would usually get after dinner on a weeknight: their choice of an apple, orange, kiwi... "Be careful your strategy doesn't backfire," she warns me in the locker room after class. "My mother's a dietitian, and she would only let us have cereals with three grams of sugar or less when we were kids."

I nod sympathetically, but I don't see a problem yet.

"And I spent the first year of college eating sugar cereals and Pop-Tarts three times a day."

"Really?" I push her.

"Well, I had the occasional blueberry muffin."

Meanwhile, Maya's gotten her hands on the brown bag and has seen what's inside. She's clapping and saying, "I like Paige!" I'm shaking my head. Then Paige says, "You can't be perfect, Betsy," and I think, Hey now, Paige, there's no need to hit below the belt.

With my new friend's admonitions ringing in my ears, I let the kids have one of the treats after dinner, even though it's a fruit dessert night, because that's the kind of mom I am — warm, fun-loving, flexible — until the next morning, anyway, when Maya looks up at me with her innocent eyes and says that "all the other kids in kindergarten" get something sweet in their lunch every day, and why can't she? Just this once? And even though I say yes, it still ends badly, because Maya doesn't want a Moon Pie, and Zack thinks she shouldn't bring a GooGoo Cluster to school because it contains peanuts and some kids are deathly allergic.

Before I can praise Zack for his thoughtful compassion, Maya suddenly bursts into tears. She is inconsolable, and I've had it. I hand the matter off to Andy and leave the room to cool down. Despite having bought them an expensive fryer and cake pan they've been wanting for weeks and even years, and despite giving them candy in their lunch boxes, my kids are still miserable and the fighting in the house continues apace. Indeed, everything's even a little worse than usual. I'm waiting for the new multivitamins with iron to work their magic on everyone's chronic fatigue and irritability (who cares if they're pale).

SHOT IN THE ARM

We're right back at square one. Seriously, why do we need to eat so well again? I forget. Is it for our health, planetary health, what? I'm losing steam and we've only just begun.

The words of the angry nutritionist ring in my ear: "Organic is not a sustainable message." And then up pipes Andy the Treacherous: "I'm worried about the elitism question. Are you just talking to an incredibly tiny part of the population as far as saving the earth or whatever the upside is supposed to be?"

Now he's on *her* side? I've always thought it was elitist to assume that organics are elitist. Their cost may be prohibitive for most people, but with just a few swipes of a pen, laws could be passed that would change that. I'm not sure where to turn for succor, but then right in the middle of this disheartening week I get an e-mail from Lionette's, a tiny market in downtown Boston that sources meats, cheeses, and produce from dozens of local food purveyors and farmers. A light dawns: I need a little pep talk from some folks who speak my language to get me back on track. I e-mail the market asking if they can spare an hour and I get a note back from one of the owners saying yes. He goes on:

> I will try to be optimistic, but I feel I am increasingly becoming a doomsayer. I truly believe we, as a society, have passed the point of no return. There is just so little outrage

over what we are offered to eat. People are so accustomed to
the cheap price of mass-produced food and refuse to pay the
real price of real food.

Look forward to meeting you.

Cheers,

Jamey Lionette

Jamey sounds anything but cheerful. Still, I'm curious about
what he'll have to say. I might come out of our meeting suicidal,
but I'm almost positive he'll buttress my commitment to sustainable eating with lots of awful facts.

I WALK INTO Lionette's Market on a seventy-degree January afternoon and Jamey is there to greet me. We head next door to Garden
of Eden, the restaurant his family also owns. A few minutes later
his brother Robert joins us. Over (imported) mineral water, the
three of us talk about the vagaries of sustainability in the twenty-
first century. Soon enough, Jamey makes big statements like, "Cap-
italism and sustainable food aren't compatible," and that when my
children grow up, they're going to be angry with me when they
realize the food supply is decimated. I'm sure he's right that they'll
be angry with me, although I'm not sure it will be about the food
supply. More likely, as my high-school friend Ethan points out, it
will be because they were éclair deprived.

We're talking about what will happen if we don't clean up
our food supply and the world in which our food is grown when
Jamey vehemently says that if we don't make changes, "Then we
don't deserve to be here and good riddance to the bad rubbish,"
by which he means human life on Earth. I start laughing, not
because I think the topic is funny — far from it — but because,
while it's true we all have our flaws, still . . . *Bad rubbish?*

A lot is going through my mind in response to this sentiment, but I can't sum it up succinctly so instead I just say, "I have kids so I have to be hopeful."

"Oh?" he says, leaning in closer. "So you're basically lying?"

"It's different once you have kids," I stammer, then turn to Robert, who has a two-year-old son. "When you're a parent you have to choose hope and joy," I say desperately. "Right?" Then I hold my breath, because Robert is the bridge. He knows as well as Jamey what we're up against as we try to make a difference, but Robert is also a dad. Doesn't he agree that everything changes once you have a child?

"Absolutely," he says emphatically, and I breathe a little sigh of relief. And though I don't say anything, I can't help notice that while Jamey may hate to compromise, he does. He sells the imported water, after all, and spinach from California, and chocolates and other sweets. It just wouldn't be possible only to carry local foods, as he'd like, and stay in business. We're all just doing our best against uneven odds. Even Jamey, who is incredibly appealing in spite of his fire. Or maybe because of it.

The afternoon, and the handsome Lionette brothers, has had its intended effect: I'm once again excited about pushing forward with our makeover. There are still a lot of questions that need answering, but at least we're on a path. I'm just hoping it doesn't wind up being a path to more family dissent.

Or, even worse, a path to warm-from-the-oven millet–cornmeal–soy milk muffins sweetened with orange juice and "a little more molasses than usual" like those Andy and I were served for a breakfast out one morning. They smelled nasty and had a metallic aftertaste. But even though we didn't eat the muffins, they were good for us in a more important way: they showed what will happen if we take this quest too far. There has to be a middle way between cake and fries on the one hand, and sugarless millet–soy milk muffins on the other.

With things back in perspective, we're ready to move on to step 2: the meat of the matter.

Chapter 3

Some Animals Are More Equal

SLIM JIM

That's disgusting," Zack says angrily, referring to the seitan Andy put in the grocery cart. "It's fake!"

"That's Daddy's," I say defensively.

"Yeah, but he's just buying it because he's trying to make you happy."

Zack may be right, but if so, it's only because somewhere along the way, Andy lost touch with his roots. He wasn't always the bacon-loving man he is today; there were a good fourteen years or so when he was a strict vegetarian. He says his unease began when he was about Maya's age and his parents took him to buy a whole side of beef in a walk-in freezer; he still remembers it with a shudder. His mom insists this is all crazy talk. "No, no, he wasn't traumatized," she says, although she also admits, "It *was* hard to eat the steak they gave us after seeing all that meat."

He reentered the land of carnivores when he was twenty-eight and living in Kansas for a month for work; lonely, bored and a little out of his mind, he ended more than a decade of meat-free living with a ConAgra Slim Jim — the one that contains "mechanically separated meat," or salvaged meat scraps that would otherwise be unusable. He went from vegetarian to dry meat snack eater in five sad minutes.

FACTORY HARM

Meat is one of the cornerstones of our makeover, and after reading *The Omnivore's Dilemma* by Michael Pollan I feel more strongly than ever that we need to eat less of it. As Pollan explains, "To visit a modern Confined Animal Feeding Operation (CAFO) is to enter a world that for all its technological sophistication is still designed on seventeenth-century Cartesian principles: Animals are treated as machines — 'production units' — incapable of feeling pain. Since no thinking person can possibly believe this anymore, industrial animal agriculture depends on a suspension of disbelief on the part of the people who operate it and a willingness to avert one's eyes on the part of everyone else."

Of course, that's exactly what Zack wishes we would do: avert our eyes. In fact, the more Andy and I discuss what's wrong with animal protein, the more of it Zack wants to eat. "Why are you so into meat lately?" I ask him, trying to sound curious and not ticked off.

"Because I'm rebelling against you," he says matter-of-factly.

Maybe this is just life with a preteen. Or maybe now that we're turning our attention to meat, Zack's getting more nervous about what the fallout will be in terms of family dinners. He doesn't want his parents to ruin his life as a happy carnivore. That's understandable. It's also too bad, because there are definitely going to be some changes around here.

Soon after finishing Pollan's book, and just to drive the point home, I come across this quote from him in an issue of *Food & Wine* magazine about what shocked him most about the American food system: "Looking at how we feed animals things that make them sick, and then give them drugs to keep them from getting too sick. Feeding chicken manure to cows and then dead cows back to chickens. The way we treat animals is shocking."

There's one more tiny thing to mention about factory-farmed meat. A 2006 policy brief from the United Nations Food and Agriculture Organization says, "Livestock production is a major contributor to emissions of polluting gases, including nitrous oxide, a greenhouse gas whose warming potential is 296 times that of carbon dioxide." Livestock production emits a greenhouse gas whose warming potential is 296 times worse than carbon dioxide? And that's in addition to methane and ammonia, other polluting byproducts of massive meat farms? "Between 1980 and 2004," the report goes on, "global meat production almost doubled."

Even if none of this bothered us, everyone also says we shouldn't eat too much anyway because it's laden with bad fat and cholesterol. What's an ethics-, earth-, and health-loving mother to do? First she makes an impassioned case against meat; eventually, though, she succumbs to the pressure and the undeniably delicious aroma of salt-and-pepper chicken wings that her husband pulls from the oven just when they've turned perfectly brown.

Apparently, while Andy says he's committed to the meat phase of our makeover, he's not exactly where he needs to be yet. Still, there have to be some remnants of the old vegetarian leanings tucked away in his brain somewhere. After all, that seitan sure as heck didn't come from me. I pull out *The Omnivore's Dilemma* and open it to chapter 17, "The Ethics of Eating Animals."

"Will you read it?" I ask calmly, sort of shoving it toward him.

"I'm a moderate," he warns, reaching out to take it.

"I know!" I say super sincerely. "And I'm not saying you'll change. Just keep an open mind." I smile at him serenely, though secretly I'm thinking, Change! Change! Change!

When he finishes reading, he looks up. I shrug somewhat apologetically; I know I'm messing with the tacit rules on which our marriage is based, although Righteous Betsy believes (no, she knows) marriage was created specifically to accommodate personal growth, even if it leads to less bacon. I get that this is a lot to ask — we all freaking love bacon — so I say, "This is really important."

He generously replies, "Then we'll make it happen."

What he doesn't know yet is that by "this," I'm referring to our entire way of thinking about food, mealtimes, shopping, and eating out. Over time, he'll come to figure that out, and he won't be happy, but for now we'll start with meat.

SOME ANIMALS ARE MORE EQUAL THAN OTHERS

"In the 1600s," the Plimoth Plantation living history museum Web site says, "Wampanoag People believed that all creatures were equal. For this reason, we did not keep any animals as pets . . . Respect for animals was also shown when the men went hunting. The Wampanoag were sure to say thank you to the Creator and to the animal itself every time they took a life . . . Another way the Wampanoag showed their thanks was to not be wasteful. In the 17th century, the People used all parts of the animal, for clothes, tools and food."

This sounds like such a wise and wonderful philosophy; unfortunately, we fail on all counts. We have a pet; we waste food; and we don't say a prayer of thanks before we eat, whether we're digging into beef or bok choy.

When I first bought Michael Pollan's book, it took me a while to start reading it, in large part because rumor had it that he wrote about killing and cooking a pig. Ultimately I gave in, and while it was an intense scene, it was also thought provoking. If we're trying to become more conscious about our diet, and if we're going to keep eating meat, then we should do the same. Getting back to basics and killing an animal would make us so much more aware of the consequences of our actions.

Only, it's just not going to happen.

Shoot a pig? I don't think so. What would Zack say? Or little Maya?

Then it occurs to me: Zack says I'm nuts. What would he think of Michael Pollan — writer, dad, pig killer? Curious to know, I tell him about Pollan's adventure, though only in the broadest strokes. I don't want to terrify the boy, just feel him out.

"That's *nasty!*" he exclaims, and I start nodding. Yes, I was right. Even without going into the gory details, Zack thinks Pollan is —

"That's *sick!*"

Wait a minute. His tone isn't quite what I'd expected. He sounds kind of . . . "I wish I could do that!" He holds his arm straight out in front of him, finger pointed at an imaginary pig, and starts making loud machine-gun noises. Then he looks at me and grins.

We need to come up with another plan. That's when Bob Sargent comes to mind. I first met Bob more than a decade ago, when he was the chef at a restaurant in Cambridge. Over the years he and his wife, Mary Jo, went from being my interview subjects to becoming friends of ours. They have owned their restaurant, Flora, for a decade now, and in the past Bob has talked about ordering whole local pigs for the restaurant. He agrees to let the four of us tag along the next time he goes to the farm to meet the pig, then see it delivered to Flora in parts, and finally, feast on it after he's worked his magic.

I'm excitedly telling Andy, who's furrowing his eyebrows. "I don't think we should bring the kids to the farm," he says flatly. Yes, it would be educational, experiential learning at its best. But neither Zack nor Maya has any interest in meeting animals that will then become their dinner. Zack's eyes grow cloudy every time he hears us talking about the pigs. Ultimately, Andy convinces me and I agree to leave the two of them behind, "in the warm safety of the classroom," as a relieved Zack puts it.

Once that's decided, Andy turns his attention to me. "I'm worried you're going to have an existential crisis," he adds. And though he doesn't say it out loud, I also know he's thinking, *What the hell will happen around here if you do? Things are wild enough already.*

"I just had one of those," I reply reassuringly. "That was chapter two."

"But you haven't met the pig yet. This could send you into extreme vegetarianism."

Andy is an understated guy; for him, this is tantamount to sending off the emergency flare. Sure, like so many people, I've dabbled with vegetarianism, but as is true for most of us, including Andy, I've ended up right back at maple-glazed pork ribs. In fact, I can't help wondering how much he's actually fretting over his *own* possible dinner crisis, because neither of us really wants to give up ribs.

PIG

And so, on a brisk Wednesday morning in January, it's just Andy and me joining Bob and his son Avery on a day trip to the Farm School, a nonprofit organization in Athol, Massachusetts, offering programs for kids, apprenticeships for adults, and an on-site, one-room middle school. In fact, it feels as though we're on a school field trip of our own.

On our drive out, Bob says he likes to do this a couple times

Family Dinners

. . . .

If you're not religious and your family won't brook an evening prayer of thanks, we've found sharing "the best part of your day" palatable to all, and it brings us to the same happy end point (a moment of acknowledged gratitude).

a year. Why pork and not another animal? "With pig, the whole thing's usable, and customers notice a difference. They'll say, 'Wow, this is great pork!' And it's profitable. I've done goats, but they're not a big seller. And if I do steak, it's really expensive *and* I'm losing profit *and* the customer goes, 'Oh, I like the other steak better.' To me," he says, "that's not a sustainable position to take," and he laughs. A few minutes later he adds, "People who support sustainability generally think it's a great idea, but when you ask them to pay for it, they say no."

How does ten-year-old Avery feel about meeting the pig that will soon become his dinner? (He's homeschooled, so this is all in a day's work for him.)

"That's a really hard question," he admits.

"Will you eat it?" I ask.

"Yeah, I guess I will," he answers hesitantly.

Bob: "If it wasn't so delicious, it would be easier to refuse."

Avery nods.

"Mary Jo has the kids thank the animal every time we eat meat," Bob says. I've tried this in the past too, saying a kind of grace at dinner, but everyone just mumbled the words and nervously made jokes, so I gave up.

"What do you say?" I ask Avery, who remains silent.

" 'Thank you, pig,' " Bob pipes up. "Right, Avery?"

"They can't hear you," Avery protests.

"It's not for them, it's for you," Bob answers, dadlike.

"Why can't you just think about it in your head?" Avery presses, and I realize that my kids aren't the only ones resisting their parents' sagacity. This makes me feel better in some small way, although this conversation has also made me want to get back on the grace bandwagon — only maybe not just yet. I'm not sure anyone's ready for any more new *ideas*.

A few minutes later we pull up to the Farm School, a fully horse-powered farm. It is, to say the least, bucolic. Within minutes, we're in the barn looking at goats. Roy S. G. Nilson, the manager and teacher, is unselfconsciously petting and sweet-talking them ("C'mere, sweetheart") while waxing rhapsodic about the tastiness of goat meat. As Roy shows us around, he introduces the animals, telling us about the personality quirks and breed and name of each one.

For years, he didn't eat meat. Strangely, that changed when he started working at the Farm School about six years ago. "People say, How can you raise them and then eat them, and I say, I do it because I love them more than anything," he explains. "In order to save these old-fashioned pig breeds, we need a market for them. We need people to eat them. We've already lost about a hundred breeds of cattle in the last hundred years." As he stops talking so he can coo over yet another barnyard beast, he adds emphatically, "I *love* these animals."

Indeed, he is so amazing to his charges that Andy and I begin to wonder: Is Roy nicer to his goats than we are to our children? We think about all the times we've yelled at Zack because right after we've told him to stop eating something — chips, say, or a

Decoding Meat Labels

According to the USDA, hormones are not allowed in raising hogs or poultry, so the claim of no hormones added to pork or chicken is meaningless. That's not the case with beef, though, where hormone use is common. And antibiotics can be used in both meat and poultry.

Find it all a little too confusing? Want to avoid hormones and antibiotics in your animal protein altogether? Buy USDA-certified organic meats and poultry.

piece of cake — he's crammed one more big bite in his mouth just to spite us. But we talk it over more and decide nah, because while Roy is affectionate to his charges, and definitely sweeter, he also eats them. "And who knows how he'd be if the animals could talk back," Andy adds.

We come out of the barn, round the corner and here they are, Bob's pigs, roaming happily in a small fenced-in area. Until a couple days ago, Roy tells us, they had free rein of the fields, but now they're confined to what is still a relatively pleasant-looking pen. The pigs are brown and tan and smaller than others we've seen. We're looking at them carefully, expecting to have a Moment; we know that pigs are extremely intelligent animals and that some people even keep them as pets.

But there's a brutal, whipping wind on the farm today, and while we're standing in front of the pen trying to be One with the pigs, they won't even glance in our direction. Somehow, these guys don't elicit the sympathy response Andy and I had feared. Andy points out that the cows are more charming and therefore more disturbing. I have to agree. They too are rare breeds, and they come over to greet us in the field. One of them even takes a few nibbles of my purse. "Will this affect your beef eating?" I ask Andy. "Too early to call," he says. "I'm not the kind of guy to make any dramatic changes. There has to be a reasonable alternative."

"And vegetables aren't a reasonable alternative?"

"Yeah, I guess so."

At the end of our visit, Bob and Roy get down to business, talking about when the pigs will be slaughtered and how Bob would like them cut up. Bob says he wants the feet, jowls, and head, which reminds me to tell him that when he's cooking the pig: no graphic-looking feet or head for us, thanks; having met the pigs is enough of an exploit for one meal, and just hearing about us meeting the pigs is enough for the kids.

DRINK YOUR MILK?

When you're on a farm and focused on a family meal makeover, there's one more issue that's impossible to ignore: milk. Many people complain that these days kids drink too much soda and not enough of the white stuff. But while no one except the companies that profit from it would argue that carbonated sugar water is okay for kids, how much dairy do they really need? I know I said we'd made our final decision about this issue months ago, but now that we've seen these sweet cows up close the thought of drinking the milk meant for their own young seems especially peculiar, even gross. Meanwhile, these cows are the lucky ones, living the life of Riley on a large pasture, carefully milked by hand every day; most dairy cows don't have it so good. We've moved on to step 3: dairy.

Walter Willett, chair of the Nutrition Department at the

Harvard School of Public Health and professor of medicine at the Harvard Medical School, says in his book *Eat, Drink and Be Healthy* that despite what both the dairy industry and the USDA food pyramid would have us believe, *milk is not a necessary food;* bone health depends more on factors like exercise, getting enough vitamin D, avoiding too much retinol (a type of vitamin A), and eating less protein, especially that found in meat. He writes, "Dairy products shouldn't occupy a prominent place in our diet, nor should they be the centerpiece of the national strategy to prevent osteoporosis. Instead, the evidence shows that dietary calcium should come from a variety of sources and, if more calcium is really needed, from cheap, no-calorie, easy-to-take supplements."

Or, I would argue, from delicious chocolate calcium candy, but I know what he's saying.

"Then you can look at dairy products as an optional part of a healthy diet and take them in moderation, if at all."

After reading this, I contact my on-call nutritionist, Dr. Roberts, to see what she thinks. She writes back, "I agree that the evidence isn't perfect. But we are a sedentary society and don't put enough pressure on our bones, so while the science gets worked out I'm personally taking calcium and drinking milk."

Milk, yes! Milk, no. Milk, yes! Milk, no . . .

We still buy milk, though, mostly because if we didn't, the kids would go wild. They like it. So, then there are a few other issues to consider— for example, hormones.

As Walter Willett writes, "Today's milk contains a more concentrated hormonal stew than it did years ago. Naturally occurring hormones in milk include estrogens and progestins, androgens, and insulinlike growth factors, to name just a few. Estrogens and progestins can stimulate breast cancer, androgens promote prostate cancer, and elevated levels of insulinlike growth factor have been linked with breast, prostate and colon cancer."

And that's without any tampering; as the cherry on top of this already pumped-up sundae, since 1994 Monsanto has been selling a genetically engineered growth hormone, called recombinant bovine somatotropin, or rbST (sometimes referred to as recombinant bovine growth hormone, or rBGH), to increase milk production. As the company writes on its Web site, "Cows supplemented with POSILAC (the brand name for rbST) produce an average of 10 lb. more milk per day."

Marion Nestle explains in *What to Eat*, "In 1993, when the FDA was considering whether and how to approve rbST, Monsanto mounted the most heavy-handed industry lobbying campaign imaginable to get the FDA to approve the drug but not require rbST milk to be labeled . . . The result: no special labeling of rbST milk. Dairies that were not using rbST, however, thought the difference would indeed matter to some consumers and that the ruling was unfair. They started labeling their products 'rbST-free.' Monsanto objected, and the FDA again agreed with the company."

Hence, we get circuitous disclaimers like the one on the milk in my fridge: "From cows not treated with rBGH. No significant difference has been shown between milk derived from rBGH treated and non-rBGH-treated cows."

Just as I'm mucking around in all of this hormone hell, Maya comes in and asks for a glass of milk.

"How about water?" I ask in a bubbly voice. She shakes her head. "Juice?" Normally juice wins out over milk all day long, but of course not this time. She shakes her head again. I try to hide my disgust as I pour just half a glass and hand it to her; then I get back to reading this on Monsanto's Web site: "Consumers — many of whom are misled by the deceptive advertising — pay higher prices for milk and get nothing in return." Though Monsanto's concern for their customers is touching, I'd like to point out that "nothing" — as in no *extra* hormone (or antibiotic) residues in our children's drink — is exactly what many of us are looking for when we buy milk. It's a shame that "nothing" costs so much more.

But at this point it makes sense that the folks at Monsanto are whining (Monsanto's board of directors needs a nice long nap): in September 2006, the *Boston Globe* reported, "The region's biggest dairies are rushing to rid their bottled milk of artificial growth hormones in a bid to draw back customers who have switched to organic milk."

Given all the above, we should probably be dairy-free, which sounds great except that would mean no more thick, creamy Greek yogurt; glorious cheese of all kinds; and bittersweet hot fudge sauce. Will this cruel makeover require us to deny our children a glass of cold milk with their warm-from-the-oven chocolate chip cookies?

The kids would find this a moot point because they never get warm-from-the-oven chocolate chip cookies. Still, once in a while they do have cookies, and those are the times we're glad we have organic milk in the fridge. Problem solved, right? Well, of course not, because, when it comes to dairy products, there are billions of dollars at stake, which means nothing about the matter will be simple.

So there can be a carton of organic milk in the fridge — a carton that Andy bought with the kids yesterday — and it can still cause a familiar tightening in my chest. Why? First of all, it's ultrapasteurized, which is a high-heat process that makes for a much longer shelf life but which some contend kills beneficial enzymes and vitamins. Plus, some also say that many of the biggest "organic" dairies, including the one that produced the milk in our fridge, are essentially factory farms that simply use organic feed.

I try to keep my voice neutral when I ask Andy about the questionable carton.

"The kids wanted milk yesterday," he replies. "What was I supposed to do?"

Sensing his exasperation, I back off and say soothingly, "I know, I'm sorry." It's not as if when we got married nearly fifteen years ago Andy knew that mealtime would become such a minefield. Then again, neither did I. After all, you'd think a glass of wholesome, pure milk would be simple. If it weren't, then all those shirtless athletes and sexy singers wouldn't pose for magazine ads wearing (disgusting, fake) milk mustaches, right? If stars drink it, it must be good. And slimming.

But maybe organic isn't the only way out; there's always raw milk to consider, which, Roy tells me, contains all sorts of good stuff—enzymes and lactase and cream on top. The Weston A. Price Foundation writes that "pasteurization destroys enzymes, diminishes vitamin content, denatures fragile milk proteins, destroys vitamins C, B12 and B6, kills beneficial bacteria, promotes pathogens and is associated with allergies, increased tooth decay, colic in infants, growth problems in children, osteoporosis, arthritis, heart disease and cancer."

But if it's not pasteurized it's, like, *raw*.

"Humans have been drinking raw milk for nearly eight millennia," Roy points out.

"Yes," I counter, "but we also used to have a life expectancy of about twenty-eight years."

"I don't think it was because of milk," Roy answers with a small smile.

I don't think so either, but how's a person to know for sure? Still, Roy and Weston A. Price are drawing me in. Raw milk sounds so healthful and so good for the kids' immune systems. We know people who drink it and they seem fine.

Then Sam Putnam comes over with his family one lazy Sunday afternoon. He is the *chef de cuisine* at Ashmont Grill in Dorchester,

Massachusetts, and a staunch advocate of a sustainable food supply. We're talking about the siren call of raw milk. "That's not safe," he warns, and suddenly I'm wide awake. You have to know for *sure* that the person supplying it is incredibly conscientious, Sam says, because if he's not, your kids could die.

Okay, got it. For now, raw milk's off the table but not without an accompanying sense of defeat. The fact that I am even considering it shows just how bad dairy has gotten. When a mom can't even pour her kids a glass of milk without encountering a political, moral, legal, health, and economic maelstrom, things have officially gone haywire.

What's a mother to do? There's a local dairy that delivers milk in glass bottles, and that seems both pastoral and lovingly old-fashioned, but the company's Web site shows more photos of machinery and delivery trucks and buildings than it does of cows grazing. The only way to know how the cows live would be to visit the farms, but this isn't an *extreme* makeover. So until Roy moves in next door and starts supplying us with safe raw milk from rare breed cows, we'll keep buying low-fat organic milk from the store — only not a half gallon as usual, but rather a quart, because in this case we've decided less is more.

We'd whip up a vegan meal in response to this grotesque dairy predicament, but when flipping through a magazine, I see vegan recipes for carrot soufflé (no), a crumbly-looking leek quiche with a whole wheat crust that uses tofu instead of eggs (no), and a carrot cake using vegan margarine (no, no, NO).

MICHAEL

Zack's friend Michael probably wouldn't like the sound of carrot soufflé either. His parents, Janet and Jon, are vegetarians (although they wisely allow their kids to eat whatever they want outside the house). So it's not surprising that Michael doesn't like meat — he loves it. I imagine when he looks at Andy and me, he sees smiling bacon where our mouths should be. We are his meat connection, and until recently, when I started learning more, we've been happy for it, though always a little embarrassed when he would tell his parents what he ate at our house: Bacon. Ribs. Steak. Still, it's satisfying watching Michael relish a meal.

So there the five of us were, celebrating Zack's tenth birthday about a year ago at the East Coast Grill in Cambridge, when Michael suddenly piped up, "Betsy, are you going to eat that?"

The server had just delivered our appetizers. I'd gotten a lone rib, shiny from a ginger-soy sauce, with a few curls of green scallion scattered on top. I'd ordered the kids some sweet, juicy watermelon, because we knew that all three of them would like it. Soon enough, though, I realized fruit wouldn't cut it for one of them.

"Are you gonna eat that?" Michael asked again, this time openly coveting my bone.

I told Michael I was, in fact, going to eat my pork rib. And then, *just to be polite,* I added, "Do you want some?"

"No, that's okay." But he couldn't take his eyes off it. A minute later, "You're gonna eat *all* of it?"

"It's one bone, Michael. I think I can handle it. But do you want a bite?"

"No, that's okay."

I was just getting ready to dig in, when he asked a third time. This time I said, "Actually no, I'm not. Go ahead, it's all yours." And I pushed the plate across the table toward him.

"Oh, no, really, no no, that's okay." Pause. "You sure?"

"I could order another one if I really wanted it. Go ahead." The only reason it took me so long to offer it up, other than greed, was the fear that it would be too spicy for him, and then it would go to waste. It wasn't, and it didn't; Michael loved that rib so much that more than a year later, the four of us still laugh at the memory of him gnawing on that bone. It just goes to show that no matter what example we set at home our kids will always follow their own path, which is usually the one that leads them farthest away from us parents.

Along with pork ribs and super-crispy bacon, there are so many other meat dishes Michael and the four of us love: thin slices of ham pan-fried until crisp; thick burgers on the grill topped with lettuce and ripe tomato slices; chicken roasted with lemon and thyme . . . I can't help wondering, though: shouldn't we be vegetarians, like Michael's parents, Janet and Jon, and like Andy and I used to be? As our friend Claire sums up so nicely, "I'm scared of meat."

("How can you be scared of *meat*?" Maya asks derisively when I share this comment over a not coincidentally vegetarian dinner. "It's just *food*." As if. But needing to cover up so that we don't have to go into unsavory details with our kindergartner, I just say, "She wants to be healthy, and meat's not always healthy."

"Oh, she's watching her figure?" Zack asks.

Watching her figure? Where'd he get *that* expression?

"Can we just change the subject?" I plead.)

WHOLE HOG

A week after our visit to the Farm School, I get a call from Bob saying that Roy and the pigs are on their way to his restaurant. By now I've wised up. I don't ask Zack if he wants to go with me, and I wouldn't even consider bringing Maya along. It's a frigid January night, too cold and late for the kids. I pull on my long down coat and race over to Flora, arriving at the back door just as the boxes of pig parts — four hundred pounds of them — are being offloaded from Roy's pickup. In the basement kitchen, Bob is pulling things out and examining them — here's a head, there's a section of fat — until he comes across an unidentifiable hunk of something fleshy and red: the heart and liver. "Oh man, that's nasty!" he says, then laughs. I'm glad I'm not the only one who thinks so.

Roy is here with another farmer from the Farm School, Mamadou Traore, known as Papis. He is from Senegal. I ask them both how it feels to drive animals to the slaughterhouse. "At first, it was tough," Roy recalls. "But now I feel relatively little remorse. As we tell the kids who visit the Farm School, if we love the animals and we want to make a place for them in the world, we need them to support us." Adds Papis, "For me, it's normal. I tell the kids, Guys, they have to be food for us to sell, so we can run the farm." Roy goes on, "We're inextricably bound. We can't do without them, and they can't live without us raising them." Roy then talks about how gentle the man at the slaughterhouse was with Bob's pigs. "It was so tidy and neat there."

We're at an unset table in the empty private dining room. Roy and Papis are not exactly dressed for eating out — not that you need to be dressed up to eat at most Boston restaurants — I'm just saying you might want to have washed the goat piss off. But they haven't had a chance to; they're clearly at the end of a long day, which included a runaway steer, an unhealthy newborn goat they're nursing back to health, and a drive to both the slaughterhouse and Flora, along with their typical daily chores and animal care. I'm asking lots of questions, the answers to which include sentences like, "Killing them could be less traumatic than removing their testicles" and "Cutting the jugular is not necessarily painful," plus the pros and cons of butchering animals with axes, knives, guns, or hammers. If I were talking to anyone else, I'd be feeling mighty uncomfortable by now.

Instead I think about how hard Roy and Papis work to keep city dwellers like us fed. And how glad I am that we're not farmers too. Get peed on by sick goats? Slit a chicken's throat? *Give*

Grilling

Grilling meat makes it taste fantastic, but unfortunately it also adds carcinogenic compounds to your dinner, including HCAs (heterocyclic amines) and PAHs (polycyclic aromatic hydrocarbons). To reduce the risk, here are some suggestions from the American Institute of Cancer Research:

- Grill vegetables, which do not produce HCAs. Good choices for grilling are portobello mushrooms, summer squash, corn, eggplant, sweet peppers, asparagus, and onions.
- Trim fat and choose lean cuts of meat to reduce drips and the resulting PAH-containing flare-ups.
- Precook meats, fish, and poultry in the oven, and then briefly grill for flavor.
- Opt for smaller cuts like kebabs, which spend less time on the grill.
- Flip meat frequently to accelerate cooking and help prevent HCAs from forming.
- Marinate meats, which some research suggests can help reduce the formation of HCAs by well over 90 percent.
- Remove all charred or burnt pieces before eating.

up take-out Thai? Unthinkable. Still, while buying cheap meat all cleaned and packaged at the store is easy, it no longer feels like a palatable choice.

Eating these pigs that we looked at — true, not in the eye, although Lord knows we tried — will be an honest act. Andy and I now know, and trust, the farmer who raised them and brought them to be killed. We don't want to be the ones raising or killing them, though, and that will never change. So yes, thank you pig for giving your life, but let's also give a big shout-out to Roy, and to the nice man who executed these pigs so humanely, and let's not forget Bob, because he's the one who will be turning these parts into something mouthwatering, bless his soul.

Indeed, that's just what he's doing when we talk on the phone the day after the delivery: making sausage, ham, pâté, and guanciale (a kind of unsmoked Italian bacon). He's going to use some of the pork loin as a weekend special, he tells me, and he plans on turning the forty pounds of belly into salty, crispy confit. None of us can wait to taste it, but we'll have to; great pork takes time to cure.

BIG PIG DINNER

Fast-forward two months. We're finally at the Sargents' house for dinner, milling around the kitchen while Bob stirs and chops and finishes dinner prep, when I ask Avery what it was like to make guanciale. "The head was sliced in half," he answers unflinchingly, "and you flipped it over so the skin was facing you. Then you cut the entire part of the face that wasn't hard or had a mouth or anything like that."

"How was that for you?" I ask, suddenly glad I wasn't the one who'd had to make guanciale. He pauses for a long enough time to unnerve the adults in the room, who can't help jumping in with suggestions — "Was it gross?" "Were you upset?" — until he finally finds his voice and answers, "It's hard to tell. It was kind of like . . . *wow.*"

"But you're ready to eat it tonight?"

"Yeah."

As we watch Bob cut the ribs apart and stir the soup on the stove, it's hard not to think back on that glacial day when we saw the pigs snuffling around at the farm. We were all concerned that knowing the pigs' provenance would ruin our appetites, but it hasn't. We're ready to dig in, which is good, because for tonight's feast, Bob has generously made no fewer than *six* different preparations of pork:

There are two types of sausage, one lightly smoked with garlic and another made with rosemary, along with grainy mustard and homemade sauerkraut on the side.

That is followed by supersmoky, falling-off-the-bone ribs. Next comes pork tenderloin that Bob had frozen and saved for tonight. He's marinated it in a sweet soy glaze and placed it atop glassy Korean noodles.

The thick white bean soup is dotted with chorizo; after he's ladled it out, Bob decadently places a square of pork belly confit on top of everyone's bowl except for Avery's, who says it's too much for him. This is a multicourse porcine extravaganza, with flavors ranging from spicy to sweet, garlicky to mild, fatty to lean. The pork is, at turns, crispy, tender, chewy, soft. As for vegetables, there are none.

I look across the table at Zack. "How is it?" I ask.

"Mmm," he answers, nodding in the affirmative. (His mouth is full.)

"Miss Maya? What do you think?"

"Eh, well," she says, then makes the so-so gesture with her hand.

"Do you like the soup?" I ask.

"I like the beans." I look at her bowl; she's been pushing the chorizo to the side.

The rest of us are devouring every greasy, filling bite of this carnivorous feast. Yes, a vegetarian diet is healthier, more ecologically sound, more humane, and cheaper. But maybe by eating much less meat of a much higher quality, we can reap most of the benefits of vegetarianism without going whole hog, so to speak. Besides, it's important to stay grounded in reality. According to the USDA, the 2005 per capita meat consumption (including red meat, poultry, and fish) was two hundred pounds. Only between 4 percent and 10 percent of the population is vegetarian, and not many people are willing to go from a couple hundred pounds of animal protein a year to zero pounds anytime soon.

Ultimately, when it comes to meat, there are two issues to consider: quality and quantity. Tonight, we got our start working on the first goal, because based on what we've learned, this pork was the zenith of what we're looking for, and while Zack and Andy both had their qualms about eating a pig we'd met when it was alive, neither of them had any trouble cleaning their plates.

As for quantity, in the car on the way home, Andy, Zack, and I realize that we're not just full of good food; we're actually overfull. We decide it was the pork belly that pushed us over the edge. We rub our own aching bellies; Andy and I even hear a small groan arising from the backseat. Of course Maya, who ate only the beans from the soup "and some of the bread," feels just fine. Which goes to show that just because the meat is as ethical, righteous, and clean as meat can be doesn't mean you should gorge yourself on it.

Chapter 3 ½

At the Table: Take 2

It's dinnertime again. Everyone's hungry, and we're ready to dig into another family meal. On tonight's menu: Caribbean Sweet Potato Gratin from *Moosewood Restaurant New Classics*. It has coconut milk, sweet potatoes, rice, spinach, and black beans. It's hearty, wholesome, vegan, and different from our usual fare.

Andy pulls the casserole from the oven; it's a gorgeous orange flecked with black beans and green spinach, all smothered by a creamy white sauce.

We serve up heaping portions for ourselves, and smaller ones for the kids. "Mmm, this is good," I say, wanting to believe it. "Zack, what do you think?"

He grimaces. "It's okay, but I don't really like it that much."

"Maya?"

"Eh, not really," she says as she carefully picks out the beans and eats them one at a time.

"How about you, babe?"

Andy: "It's okay." I have to agree. It's all style over substance. Despite its beauty, the flavors never meld; instead, it's like getting a taste of canned coconut milk, followed by sweet potato, then bitter spinach, then a bite of bland bean. It's jarring. It's bad.

The next day I pull the leftovers from the fridge. "I wonder how this will taste now," I say.

"A day older," Andy replies. He's right; it hasn't magically improved. A couple minutes later, the leftovers get tossed.

It's a sad ending to an honest attempt to take our meat consumption to the next level by eating less of it. There's no denying the dish was missing something. Was the sweet potato undercooked? Was the top too mushy? We're trying to figure it out when Andy's eyes light up and he says, "I know; how about *Moosewood* plus bacon?" Right. Our healthful vegan meal was lacking nothing other than meat.

So we decide to pick out another *Moosewood* dish; this time it'll be Thai Noodle Salad with coconut milk, garlic, ginger, lime, and mint along with snow peas, green beans, and water chestnuts. It sounds good, but we don't want to make the same mistake, so we take the liberty of tossing just the barest smattering of cubed chicken on top — one cut-up breast for six servings.

Truly free-range poultry turns out to be one of the hardest things to source, at least where we live, and we haven't figured out where we can affordably do that yet. Instead, tonight's chicken is Bell & Evans. Precooked. Maya takes a nibble of a lone noodle and says, "It's okay, but I think I better have something else to eat too." And then she sighs loudly. As I hand a bowl to Zack, he mumbles, "Chicken." As in, he wants more of it. Then he asks, "What's all that creamy-looking weirdness?" He takes a few bites of the noodles. "Is there anything else to eat?"

"There's another chicken breast in the fridge," Andy genially replies.

"Yeah, I'll have some of that."

If all this isn't enough, the kids also ask for milk. Andy and I were discussing dairy with friends one day when Zack overheard and worriedly asked, "Does this mean we have to drink less milk?"

He must not have realized that they already were; by keeping mum about it, we've managed to halve the kids' dairy consumption without their even noticing. It's been easy; instead of asking if they want milk, we offer water. If they insist, we pour half a glass. It sounds simple, but this two-pronged approach works often enough to make a difference.

After all, we're still living in a land where meat and milk rule, and the kids will never let us forget it.

Chapter 4

. . . .

Easier Said Than Done

Why do you eat watermelon if it's not in season?" my interrogator asks. I'm ready to launch into a detailed reply based on hours of research when I think, Eh, never mind. It's all too complicated, especially because my questioner is *six*. She's a friend of Maya's over for a playdate, asking about the snack I've just served. Getting into the whole story seems a bit much.

Meanwhile, she eats a whole bowlful of the melon.

I knew that everyone was talking about eating locally these days. I just didn't know that "everyone" included kindergartners. But I guess it makes sense that parents are talking to their kids about this stuff, because we all want to teach our children healthy dietary habits that will last a lifetime, and there's nothing better than eating locally and in season. That's when food not only tastes extra fresh and vibrant, but it's also more nutritious and supposedly even better for the environment because it hasn't been shipped across continents.

It's probably safer too. Every year an estimated seventy-six million Americans get sick from foodborne illnesses, and thousands die. A *New York Times* article in May 2007, "Food Imports Often Escape Scrutiny: A Problem Linked to Globalization," quoted a former assistant commissioner at the FDA as saying, "If people really knew how weak the FDA program is, they would be shocked." Or as former FDA commissioner David Kessler said before Congress in May 2007, "Simply put, our food safety system is broken."

So as the fourth step in our great meal makeover, Andy and I will transform our family of four into locavores, or people who only eat foods grown within a couple hundred miles of where they live. Novelist Barbara Kingsolver and her family did it. They spent a year living off the land in Virginia's Appalachian mountains, and then she wrote a book about the experience. "It was so much more fun than we expected it to be," she told the *New York Times*.

Her kids thought eating locally was fun? That's great; I bet ours will feel the same way. As a way to broach the subject, I tell Zack about Kingsolver's book. "Could they use stuff that was already in their house, like flour and spices?" he asks. "If they couldn't, that would be a waste, to throw out all those spices, unless they put them away for the year and saved them." That's a good point, though we don't know the answer. Neither Andy nor I have read the book yet, but we do know they were each allowed to choose one nonlocal luxury item. "Could they choose chocolate?" They could, we answer.

He nods.

"That wouldn't be too bad then," he concludes. "I'd just move in with one of my friends for the year."

Okay, we've identified the first problem with becoming locavores: the kids. Until now, our makeover hasn't affected dinnertime as much as they'd feared. Yes, we're eating less meat, although Zack can still have his beloved, overcooked steak once in a while. But being New England locavores will totally cramp their style. "What mother would deprive her children of fruit?" Zack asks derisively.

Nevertheless, we've decided to pull this off, and it should be easy, as long as from now on we employ forethought and planning, freezing and canning. Oh, and a live-in nanny — no, make that two. Plus a kindly grandmother living next door, along with a street full of friends to entertain the kids. And a personal chef. Come to think of it, there's a little something else standing in our way: it's February in New England. There hasn't been anything growing here since the fall, and there won't be for months to come.

Times like this are when my darker self emerges. Now she starts whispering, "Locabore, locasnore. Eating within a hundred mile radius is a locachore." The people who started the locavore movement live in San Francisco, not Boston; Barbara Kingsolver lives in southern Virginia, not New England. Plus, locavores tend to use funny words like *foodshed*.

INSPIRED

But then Tony Maws comes to mind. Tony's the nationally acclaimed owner of Craigie Street Bistrot in Cambridge, Massachusetts. He's such a stickler for sustainable that he changes his menu nightly. He even cops to "tormenting his suppliers" to get the ingredients he wants. How does he make the whole local-in-winter thing work?

Andy and I decide we'd better find out, and since we're about to celebrate an anniversary, and since Craigie Street Bistrot isn't exactly kid-friendly, we'll see what's what at the restaurant without Zack and Maya. Sometimes, we think as we kiss them goodnight and head out to the car, it's not so terrible that there are places where the preteen set doesn't fit in.

A couple minutes after we sit down at a table for two, we order kir royales, the official aperitif of our honeymoon. Our drinks arrive about one minute after we ordered them. We look up in surprise. "Someone overheard you wanting them," our server explains. We thought, Damn, we should have been wanting help with the laundry instead. But while we haven't learned a whit about wintertime sustainability yet, the evening is off to a fine start.

A "gratin of celery root with late fall vegetables glacées, mousseron mushrooms, black quinoa, and savory beet jus" later, it's clear that Tony is a mad genius. Not only is this dish gorgeous, with more colors than we knew were available in the winter vegetable world, but it is also downright delicate. Best of all, it's vegetarian, with lots of vegetables and whole grains. (As we're digging in, I can just hear Zack: "Where's the meat?" This has become his favorite refrain whenever we're serving less meat than usual. I'm extra glad he's not here. Nothing personal.) Just to make sure dinner hasn't been a delicious fluke, and even though we're already stuffed, we order a "gingerbread pain perdu with candied vegetables and ginger ice cream." The gingerbread is crispy and warm. The cold, spicy ice cream is the perfect foil, and the candied vegetables are like sweet, colorful gems.

This is how Boston winters could taste, if only we had Tony in our home kitchen. We're inspired. The time has come to hunt down local foods. We mean *hunt* metaphorically, of course, since we will not be trekking out to cold forests and oceans but rather driving to charming farm stands and markets.

Verrill Farm, which supplies a number of top Boston restaurants, has its homegrown harvest calendar posted on its Web site. It stops after December and starts up again in April, leaving right now blank. I call anyway to see if despite what the calendar says, there might be anything in their larder left over from last fall; the woman who answers says that in fact there is — carrots.

"That's all?"

"We also have beets," she concedes.

Right. Beets aren't really worth a mention, at least not if you ask Andy and the kids. But carrots and beets sound good to me — they're a start anyway. And Tony had turned beets into a gorgeous "savory jus" that made even the quinoa sitting on top of it seem dazzling. Then again, he's a master chef, our kids don't do beet jus, and Verrill Farm is about a thirty-minute drive away. Does it really make sense to drive half an hour for a few root vegetables that won't get eaten? Of course not, but we're going to anyway.

SUPPORTIVE

Before we go anywhere, though, we need help, because aside from the meager offerings at Verrill Farm, we don't know where to shop. I call Ilene Bezahler, editor of *Edible Boston,* a magazine that features local foods. If anyone has the inside scoop, she does. Not surprisingly, she tells me that "it's really hard this time of year to find local food," but she does give me a couple good leads on lesser-known markets and farms.

She then shares a story about an older couple who are regulars at a restaurant in Brookline, Massachusetts. Every week, she says, they order a green salad with tomatoes. The server explains why they don't have tomatoes during the winter. "How can you not have tomatoes?" the woman asks. After repeating this same scene for weeks on end, one night the couple orders a salad and doesn't ask for a tomato. The server is thrilled, thinking she's finally gotten through to them. She brings the salad to the table; the woman pulls a tomato out of her purse.

Is Ilene that strict? She'll *never* have a tomato if it's out of

---

Local Foods

To find local foods in your area, check out these sites:

www.foodroutes.org
www.eatwellguide.org
www.localharvest.org
www.ediblecommunities.com

To find information about farmers' markets, visit
www.ams.usda.gov/farmersmarkets

---

season? Well, she says, she has tomato sauce and soup in the freezer that she made last summer, but otherwise, yes, she'll wait half a year to buy any fresh. So what fruit does she eat in winter? "Citrus," she says. "That's pretty much it." Would she ever buy strawberries in winter?

"Oh, no," she replies hastily.

"Us either," I say, and mean it with all my heart.

(The next day we make dinner for friends who have come upon hard times. Jeff broke his leg playing hockey and is completely laid up; meanwhile, his wife, Robin, had flown to Kentucky to adopt a stray dog two weeks earlier — a story for another day — and the dog cut his foot on an icy Boston sidewalk and needed surgery. When Robin arrives to pick up dinner, she is limping because she just sprained her ankle. Her family needs much more than a meal, but soup is all we can offer. I made corn and crab chowder because it's easy; it's even easier if Andy buys the ingredients when he's on the road for work.

"Oh, and why don't you pick up some fruit salad?" I casually mentioned as he was walking out the door that morning. As I was divvying up the fruit between our two families — colorful, sweet, juicy watermelon and pineapple and strawberries and blueberries and cantaloupe, all of it from God-knows-where and grown who-knows-how — my swimming-lesson buddy, Paige, came to mind. "Some things," she'd once said, "you just don't want to know." Paige, I thought, when you're right, you're right.

Of course, after dinner I suffer from a guilt hangover. From now on, I promise myself, we will really stop buying fruit from faraway lands. A few days later, I get an e-mail from a magazine editor: she wants me to come up with recipes for slush and pudding using fresh cherries. They cost eight bucks a pound and hail from Venezuela. The kids are thrilled. In the end, they love the two desserts, but they actually fight over the handful of leftover cherries. Fruit deprivation isn't pretty.)

As I'm talking with Ilene, I realize that she hasn't mentioned anything about having kids. How would Zack and Maya react if we told them they could only have oranges until June? And what would the nutritionist, Dr. Roberts, say? What about the family aspect of eating locally?

"It's really hard," Ilene admits, "a major effort," and I'm nodding on the other end of the phone. But then the shoring up stops and the gauntlet gets thrown down when she shares a story about a mom who picks up raw milk from a farm every two weeks and special-orders all her groovy meat.

"So this woman has kids and she's doing all that?" I press. But then Ilene says incongruously, "Well, she doesn't give them candy." I'm not sure how that relates, but now that she's said it, it's hard not to wonder — who is this superwoman?

"And," Ilene goes on, "she grinds her own flour. She home-schools. Actually," she says, dropping her voice conspiratorially, "she really seems neurotic about food." There we have it. The woman whose example I'll never live up to is not the woman I want to become anyway.

After discovering a handful of places to check out west of Boston, Andy and I realize that sourcing enough ingredients for even one dinner could take an entire day and a whole tank of gas; once we've made that meal, it's quite possible that no one in the house but me would eat it.

CSA

If we were doing this experiment with locavorism last winter, we'd be in much better shape. That's because to stave off the usual returning-to-the-grocery-store depression, we joined a winter CSA, which stands for community supported agriculture. The idea is that you pay for a season's share of produce before the growing season is under way, thereby helping farmers keep the whole tenuous, weather-dependent business of growing our food feasible, if only barely. Our goal was to support local agriculture and eat fresh food that had been organically grown even in winter. It didn't turn out quite as well as we'd hoped.

When that first Thursday pickup arrived, the kids and I bounded out to idyllic Lincoln, Massachusetts. We came home

Community Supportive Agriculture

To find CSAs and get information about sustainability, organics, local foods, and more from the Alternative Farming Systems Information Center, go to www.nal .usda.gov/afsic.

with bag after bag full of local organic goodness: beets, parsnips, four kinds of squash, celery root, turnips, rutabaga . . . It was a giddying abundance of food, a root vegetable cornucopia. Andy, who would only eat the onions, carrots, and potatoes, was not amused.

It was up to me to stay cheerful, focused, and on task. We carefully unloaded the bags, washed the vegetables (they were so . . . *earthy*), and put them away, either in a basket on the counter or in the fridge, which we'd cleaned to make room for the new tenants. We tirelessly used up the greens in those first rosy days, then methodically moved on to the potatoes. We made slow but steady progress in reducing the pile. I felt proud.

Next, we came up with a plan for the squash: baked goods. Zack had tried pumpkin pie earlier in the fall and, much to our surprise, loved it. We'd start with pumpkin pie and move on from there to breads, cakes, muffins. We'd make them all from scratch! Put us on the prairie and we'd be just fine. Our pie was a two-day process but *so* worth it. We baked the pumpkin, let it cool, puréed it, and put it in the fridge. The next day, we mixed the filling, par-cooked the crust, and put it all together. The kids were so excited. That night, Andy and I went out for dinner, leaving Zack, Maya, and our sitter, Stacia, with the freshly baked pie, along with money to get pizza delivered, because, what, we were supposed to make pie *and* dinner?

When Andy and I got home from our date, we couldn't wait to find out: How was it? Well, Stacia said, as soon as dinner was over the kids had asked, Is there *anything else* for dessert?

Things only went downhill from there. Our cabinet on the back porch was filled with root veggies from the farm. A couple weeks later, after the first frost, I went to grab a squash, only to find that it was frozen. (No squash fights for us that night.) Then,

after the next pickup, tired, losing steam, neither Andy nor I ever
got around to washing one bag of produce. Two weeks later: mush.
We had a blessed three-week hiatus from the farm over the holidays; when we ran into the farmer at the next pickup, he asked if
we'd had enough veggies to last the extra week. It took everything
in me not to ask him if he was kidding.

So this year, we took a pass on the winter CSA. However, now
we're feeling regretful — why didn't we just sign up for half a
share, or split one with another family? But it's too late; instead,
we have to get creative.

OUT IN THE COLD

"The kids will think this is so cool, right?" I ask Andy excitedly.
Funny, he seems to think that making them miss Saturday-
morning cartoons to buy local root vegetables that will go into
dishes they'll hate is not such a good idea. He strongly suggests
we leave them at home.

I stubbornly ask Zack anyway. "Don't you think it would be
great?" He smiles and silently shakes his head. No. Which is how
Andy and I find ourselves using precious babysitting time to go
food shopping. It's not the first time this has happened, but it
seems like an especially bitter pill today. After all, this was supposed to be a whole family endeavor. Don't our kids know fun
when they see it?

Our first stop is Wilson Farms in Lexington, Massachusetts.
We corner an employee and explain our plan; he escorts us to
every local item they have on hand. We're happily surprised by
what we find — apples, honey, cider, two kinds of cheese, smoked
salmon, eggs, milk, and butter. The kids will eat every single thing

we find, as long as the cellared apples are perfectly blemish-free, that is, and as long as we don't attempt to get Maya to eat smoked fish, or Zack to try the cheese.

But we still don't have root vegetables yet, and what's local in a New England winter without a few tubers? So next stop: Arena Farms in Concord. We pick up the one tired spaghetti squash left, along with a handful of turnips. Feeling better now that we have a few roots in our satchel, we head out to our last stop, Verrill Farm, also in Concord, where we come upon fat yellow and orange carrots, those multicolored beets the woman on the phone had told me about and, as a bonus, knobby celery root. That's what we're talking about.

I feel kind of high by the time we leave Verrill Farm — we found so much more than we expected! — although that slightly "wow" feeling could also be due to a drop in blood sugar because it's been a while since I've eaten. Regardless, by the time we finish gathering all our midwinter local provisions, the euphoria is decidedly wearing off.

I'm remembering the final week of last winter's CSA, when the kids threw themselves on the living-room floor and refused to get up. Then, once I'd finally dragged them to the farm and back (using a combo carrot/stick approach), they wouldn't eat most of what we'd gotten anyway. Is this pursuit in vain? And even if it isn't, who has time for all this?

Andy the Good says he knows how to get the kids onboard with the likes of beets and celery root: "I'll fry 'em!"

"Would *you* try beets and celery root if they were fried?" I ask skeptically.

"Probably not," he admits. But for better or worse, depending on whom you ask, Andy won't have to break out the fryer after all because I come up with a different strategy: invite friends over, because other families like beets, right? Someone besides me has to.

SOUP'S ON

I call my health-conscious friend Cale — the one who's totally, even nauseatingly on top of her parenting game — and invite her and her family over for a midwinter meal. We serve spaghetti (packaged, because last time I checked no one was growing organic semolina in greater Boston) and tomato sauce (jarred, because it's not worth making homemade only for myself), along with light, soft meatballs made from some of the Lionette's ground beef (local, humane, expensive). Talk about an easy crowd pleaser; everyone digs in. Except for Maya, of course, who eats plain pasta, and Andy, who has meatballs (only because he made them) but no sauce. Cale and I both love the colorful rainbow beet and blue cheese salad (all local) with walnuts and a Dijon-tarragon vinaigrette (so not local, but even I know that beets need gussying up). No one else will even try it.

For dessert the kids and I make a butternut squash pie; it's creamy and smooth, with a kick from ginger and cinnamon, and not too sweet. The next day Stacia says it's the best thing she's ever eaten, although neither her boyfriend nor Andy will try so much as a sliver, even after that rave. Is squash pie too feminine? And is Stacia getting enough to eat lately?

A few days later, it's celeriac bisque for dinner. We've tried cooking with celeriac before, with unhappy results, but this time the velvety soup is a hit — at least with Andy, Zack, and me. Maya has pasta. The spaghetti squash looks dry inside, and indeed none of us eat it. "If we were deep in Pilgrim times," says Andy, "it'd taste like caviar." (We're not — yet. That will come later.)

Thankfully, the acorn squash is too soft, so we have to throw it out, and for dessert we have farmers cheese blintzes with local mixed berry jam on top — "The first bite was a little cheesy, but then it was *good,*" says Maya; Andy and Zack won't try them — which leaves only turnips and carrots to polish off. They go into a roasting pan along with one of the Lionette's whole chickens, as well as some organic thyme and salt (origin unknown), and organic olive oil from Spain (just try and tell me we shouldn't have it in the house). Beyond delectable.

A few days later, Andy arrives home with a care package of white paper-wrapped ham, pork shoulder, steak, hamburger, bacon, and eggs. To me, this raw, frozen meat is better than two-dozen long-stem roses. And while it takes more effort to pull off a meal with frozen local meat — once you've gone to the farm to get it, you still have to deal with defrosting — it makes everyone happy. Zack gets his steak and two loving parents; Andy gets both bacon and a content wife; I get a healthier family and world; Maya gets pasta, as usual. Eating this meat transforms a typical meal into more of a feast.

For two of us, anyway, which Andy and I realize on the night we serve some of this wonderful farm-bought pork stir-fried with organic sesame oil, organic soy sauce, and cashews. The pork has soaked up all the good flavor of the marinade; the cashews add a buttery, crunchy contrast. The four of us are gathered inside our cozy house eating while a storm rages outside. This moment proves that locavorism is not only doable but also —

"Ewww, agh, *blech!*" It's Zack, spitting out a piece of the exorbitantly expensive pork. "Fatty!" he says angrily, then mutters,

"Stupid pig ate too much." The rest of the meat on his plate goes untouched as he eats the organic brown basmati rice and stir-fried vegetables. (Maya has rice, baby corn, and water chestnuts for dinner.) I can't say I'm heartbroken.

In spite of all the forces lined up against us, nothing can slow us down. For now we'll have to satisfy our urge to eat locally with meat and tubers, but by next year, with a freezer and jars at our disposal, the sky will be the limit. Maybe we can get a recipe for candied beets from Tony Maws and see if that helps the kids see things our way.

Loco — I mean locavorism — here we come.

FAIR ENOUGH

Our experiment begat a week's worth of surprisingly colorful and tasty meals. Still, it was frustrating that not one dish went over with all four family members. Also, it was in no way a *sustainable* way to eat. It had been way too expensive, and though we'd like to keep this from Zack, scrounging up locally grown produce in the middle of a New England winter was not that much fun. Coffee, bananas, chocolate, and sugar? Now those are fun, although it's also true that nothing could be more tropical (i.e., farther from Boston).

Wait a minute. Isn't the world a global village? Because bananas are one of the six foods Maya will still eat.

Andy can't have coffee? You tell him.

And all of us are supposed to give up chocolate and sugar? *Shut up.*

As a mocha latte lover, Zack would not be amused. Yes, I've been letting Zack drink lattes ever since giving "open parenting" a try. Zack and Maya were in the middle of a school break (as usual) and the three of us were having a heck of a time hitting an assortment of vacation hot spots — the art store, the bowling alley — when I was overcome by a craving for a latte. Normally, wanting to set a good example, I'd just forgo the pleasure until the kids weren't with me, but this time, throwing caution to the wind, I dragged them into a nearby bakery and said they could each have a cookie while Mommy got herself a drink.

"Really?" Maya asked in disbelief, and before I could change my mind, she quickly pointed to a heart-shaped number covered with red sugar. But Zack didn't want a cookie. Zack wanted a latte. I hadn't considered that possibility. "Decaf is fine," he then said earnestly, and I thought, Eh, what the hell. It's too expensive and it's setting a bad precedent, but what can I do. I ordered the cookie and two decaf mochas. The nice woman behind the counter asked, "One is for him?" looking at Zack. He was probably eight at the time. I nodded.

"Wouldn't he rather have a hot chocolate?" she asked me, and then when I shrugged indifferently — I figured that all things considered, a decaf mocha was probably no worse than hot cocoa and maybe even a little better – she appealed directly to Zack: "Wouldn't you rather have a hot chocolate?" And when he said no, and I didn't make him change his order, she gave me a little tsk-tsk under her breath, then went off to foam milk. Okay, so admittedly Zack went through an intense latte phase for a few months after this. The good news, though, is that now, while he still likes them, his fervor has waned, thereby proving the moderationists right yet again.

Still, while these days I only get lattes when the kids are on school property, something's been bothering me recently. Aren't coffee, chocolate, and sugar associated with poverty and misery? Should Zack and I give up lattes forever? The urgency of these questions brings us directly to step 5 of our makeover: fair trade.

According to the Fair Trade Foundation based in London, "By requiring companies to pay above market prices, Fairtrade addresses the injustices of conventional trade, which traditionally discriminates against the poorest, weakest producers. It enables them to improve their lot and have more control over their lives."

Or how about this from an Oxfam report titled "Rigged Rules and Double Standards: Trade, Globalisation and the Fight Against Poverty": "In the globalised world of the early twenty-first century, trade is one of the most powerful forces linking our lives. It is also a source of unprecedented wealth. Yet . . . increased prosperity has gone hand in hand with mass poverty and the widening of already obscene inequalities between rich and poor. World trade has the potential to act as a powerful motor for the reduction of poverty, as well as for economic growth, but that potential is being lost."

That's enough. Andy and I decide to become supporters of a more equitable worldwide system of trade by searching out a couple suppliers stateside and placing some orders. Translation: time for some coffee and chocolate. We order some organic, fair-trade, very nonlocal commodity foodstuffs online: five pounds of whole bean Moka Java (for Andy), plus five pounds of sugar (for me and the kids). The total, including shipping, is fifty-two bucks. Expensive, but about the same as (if not cheaper than) the same amount of premium coffee and sugar would cost, and this stuff is better. We think. Besides, the coffee will last for months; the sugar, a year or longer since, much to the kids' disappointment, I haven't been baking any homemade desserts lately.

Fair Trade

. . . .

To buy fair-trade items online or to find retailers,
visit either the Fair Trade Federation at www.
fairtradefederation.org or Trans Fair USA at www
.transfairusa.org.

The second Saturday in May is World Fair Trade Day,
celebrated by people in more than seventy countries
according to the Fair Trade Federation. For more
information go to www.wftday.org.

The package arrives a couple days later. It's kind of a thrill to
receive a box of coffee and sugar in the mail. It's also a little overwhelming, because while the crinkly brown sacks of coffee and
sugar are appealing, they're also *large*. Where will we store them?

But ordering was so easy that a couple mornings later when
everyone else is off to school and work, I stealthily visit another
Fair Trade Federation member's Web site and click on four chocolate bars, wild rice, cashews, olive oil, and tea. This has kind of
turned into an online shopping frenzy, and while some might say
that no one technically *needs* these items, those people may not be
displaced mid-Atlantic natives trying to stay cheerful during yet
another seemingly endless New England winter. Besides, wild rice
is brimming with nutrients of some kind or another, olive oil is
full of good fat, and Andy and I have to have our morning coffee
and tea no matter what. The cashews, with their naturally high
iron content, seal the deal, because we still keep forgetting to give
the kids their vitamins.

After ordering, I read the Web site's privacy policy only to find

in small print in the middle of the page that this supposedly pro-
gressive company will be selling my address to other marketers
unless I opt out. I immediately shoot off an e-mail, only to keep
getting "error" messages and having my notes returned. I bet they
don't experience any errors when they're selling my e-mail address
to their "partners."

But all is forgotten when the box arrives late on a Friday afternoon. Could it really be this easy to improve the lives of families
around the world? Just a little online shopping and we're doing
our part?

O Lord, I think, please let fair trade be straightforward. But of
course it's not to be; naturally there are naysayers out there too.
Some critics claim that setting a price floor encourages overpro-
duction, thereby flooding the market in the long term and setting up a cycle of poverty that will never be broken. Then there
are those who say that fair trade as it stands doesn't go nearly far
enough if the goal is to equalize the international trade playing
field.

Fair trade is a complex system — one Oxfam report goes into
258 pages' worth of details — and it might take a PhD in econom-
ics to fully grasp all the issues. And in the end the report concludes, "Making trade work for the poor implies a broad agenda
for reform, extending from national governments up to the World
Trade Organisation." Reconfiguring international trade is more
than we can handle right now. Actually, so is the laundry.

Confused, I e-mail someone at Oxfam America, an international aid organization that conveniently has its headquarters
right here in Boston. I'll be able to get all my questions answered
within a couple days. Two weeks and about a half-dozen e-mails
and calls later, I have yet to talk to anyone at Oxfam — even just

to set up an interview. Failing to crack the code and get some answers from the behemoth that is Oxfam America — *to find out more about their own Make Trade Fair campaign* — leaves both Andy and me more than a little disillusioned. Still searching for someone to interview, I then contact not one, not two, but three other companies and organizations. None of them respond. Could the critics be right, at least in part? Is fair trade more red tape than real change?

Given all the criticisms maybe we should forget the whole thing and go back to cheap chocolate, coffee, and sugar. Before making any rash decisions, we decide to take one last stab at it by watching the documentary *Black Gold*. True, it's not the same as talking to a real person, but apparently it'll have to do.

The bottom line — there's just no way to sugarcoat this — is that low coffee prices translate into hardworking farmers who can't provide their children with clean water, warm clothes, an education, or even enough food. One farmer says that getting paid $.57 *per kilo of coffee* "would change our lives — we would soar above the sky." (A large "orange crème frapuccino" from the neighborhood Starbucks rings in at $4.65.) The film says that "over the last twenty years, Africa's share of world trade has fallen to one percent. If Africa's share of world trade increased by one percentage point it would generate a further seventy billion dollars a year — five times the amount the continent now receives in aid."

Coincidentally, just after we resign ourselves to figuring this out on our own is exactly when Adrienne Fitch-Frankel, economic justice campaigner at Global Exchange in San Francisco, calls back. She says that while the certification system may not be perfect, fair-trade farms are audited annually by independent groups. Child slavery, abuse, and poverty, she adds, "is the easiest thing in the world to address as a consumer" — just look for the fair-trade label. "Improving children's welfare is one global crisis that we have the solution to, and all you have to do is eat chocolate," she goes on.

If only it were so simple. (And thank God the kids didn't overhear this conversation.) Still, buying fair trade does seem to make sense, at least in the short term. And in the long term? An international economic overhaul to eliminate poverty worldwide. Though the cost for fair-trade items is higher, the impact on peoples' lives is huge if you listen to the farmers who speak out in *Black Gold*.

We're listening, which is why we now buy all our sugar, coffee, tea, and chocolate from online fair-trade stores. Not only do we feel great about all the families we're (hopefully) supporting, we love it when the UPS guy pulls up in front of the house.

In fact, a delivery arrives one day when the kids are at school. "What's in the box?" Zack asks interestedly when he gets home. "Oh, just tea," he says dejectedly. Clearly the time has come to impart a little life lesson. After briefly going into the issues at hand, I finish up by saying, "And so, even if I want coffee, if it's not fair trade I won't buy it."

"Wow, that's a big sacrifice," he says evenly.

"Excuse me?" I ask. Did I detect sarcasm even though we're talking about starving children?

"I'm just saying, not getting coffee is not that big of a deal, Mom." Of course he's right, although only buying fair-trade chocolate, coffee, and sugar isn't always easy, especially when we're out of the house. Besides, Zack may scoff when it comes to my mocha lattes, but what would happen if we told the kids they couldn't have standard chocolate or sugar from now on? It would decimate

Halloween in one fell swoop, not to mention brownies and basically all other desserts. (Something to consider.)

In the end, preteen mockery won't even come close to derailing this train. As Andy and I sip our morning drinks, we think of all the children out there who aren't nearly as lucky as our two troublemakers. Fair trade may be imperfect, but for now it's all we've got.

Chapter 4 ½

· ·

At the Table: Take 3

I t's Tuesday, fruit dessert night. We've just finished dinner and everyone's still sitting at the table when I bring out apple slices — Granny Smiths from across the country, stripped of both their "food-grade wax" peel and any potentially controversial brown spots. Then, just to shake things up, I also place one tiny square of chocolate in front of each of the kids. This is a two-tiered experiment involving both dark chocolate and fair trade.

First of all, Andy and I have decided to see if by treating dark chocolate as a fruit dessert condiment, in the same way we're using meat these days, the kids will accept it into their lives in place of milk chocolate. According to the BBC, a few years back researchers from Italy and Scotland found that dark chocolate boosted blood antioxidant levels by nearly 20 percent; sadly for Zack and Maya, the same effects were not derived from either dark chocolate milk or milk chocolate bars.

Zack takes one look at the small bar in front of him, then sucks in his breath and says dramatically, "Could it be true?"

Maya: "What?"

Zack: "Mom gave us chocolate."

"I didn't get any," she says accusingly.

"Yes you did, it's right in front of you," I point out.

"Oh, there it is. I didn't see it because it's so small." She's not busting chops; it really is tiny. But hey, it's still chocolate on a weeknight.

How is it?

"It's good," Zack says. "If it was milk I'd be eager for it, but I'll settle for this."

Maya: "I think it's pretty good, but it's a little bitter." She wrinkles her nose but continues to eat it.

Zack asks for more. Feeling generous, I give them both a second bar. Andy and I understand that there may be fallout from this in the form of nightly requests for chocolate from now on. But our fears are allayed when they end up devouring the apple slices too.

Even better, Maya asks, "Is it fair trade?"

"Yes."

"Yay, fair-trade chocolate!" she cheers.

Me, curious: "What do you know about fair-trade chocolate, My?"

"Nothing. But I know you like it, right?"

Zack: "It's not better than the regular stuff tastewise, but I'll take your word fair trade is better for other reasons."

It becomes apparent he actually means this when one Sunday morning he says he and Maya want to make chocolate-dipped mint leaves; do we have any fair-trade milk chocolate in the house? This clues us into three things: (1) that to the kids it's never too early for chocolate; (2) while Zack does nothing but mouth off when either of us gives him our little talks about things like poverty and international trade, the information sinks in nonetheless; and (3) apparently we haven't lectured him quite enough on the virtues of dark chocolate.

Before I've had a chance to respond, he goes on disingenuously, "If we had any, where would it be? Oh yes, I think I know: in this box, where you hide it, or else here in this container, where you also hide it." He's grinning. He's also right. We make a mental note to find better hiding spots. And while there isn't any plain milk chocolate in what we thought was our secret stash, there is a bar of fair-trade milk chocolate with hazelnuts.

"Can we use this?" he asks, holding it up. Defeated, I nod my assent. The kids proceed to overheat it until it seizes; Zack tries to salvage it by adding low-fat milk; it turns into a chocolate clump they call pudding; the clump sits in the fridge until the next day; I throw it out. So in this case, I got to be Nice Mom, they didn't eat chocolate on a Sunday morning — all's well that ends well, except for the waste.

Chapter 5

. . . .

Fishy

RAW

Do I eat fish when I'm eating sushi?" Maya asks. The four of us are in the car on our way home from a Japanese restaurant.

"You mean ikura?" Andy clarifies, since that's the only sushi she eats. Actually, it's also the only seafood she eats.

"Yeah," she says.

For some unknowable reason, Maya loves salmon roe. Obviously we'd prefer that she eat regular old fish instead, but she won't. "I'll only eat it if it's called Dora fish," she cheerily informs me one evening when I try to get her to take a bite of wild salmon.

"It is!" I lie with a big grin.

"No, it's not," she says knowingly. Then, inspecting my offer of one tiny sliver of fish with a grimace, she shakes her head and turns away.

So Maya won't eat healthy, cooked salmon, but she'll eat raw fish eggs as often as possible. We can't even remember how this started but now she's a full-blown fanatic. Wondering if it's all right for a five-year-old to eat salmon roe, I checked in with Dr. Roberts. "Not on my watch," she said. "My thirteen-year-old begs for sushi and we have a twice-a-year rule due to my concerns about raw fish risks; it has the potential for things like parasites." Enough said.

So, when on our way home from the restaurant Maya asks Andy if ikura is fish, I urgently whisper, "Tell her." He knows what I'm saying so he clearly replies, "It's fish *eggs*."

"Raw," I add.

"Really?" she asks, sounding shocked, and I think, we've done it. We've finally turned her off to ikura. Then she adds, "Awesome!"

OTHER THAN THAT, MRS. LINCOLN . . .

Maya may not eat seafood, but lots of kids do; indeed, pollock, comprising most fish sticks and patties, has been one of the top-selling fish in this country for years. Fortunately, according to KidSafe Seafood, a program of the ocean conservation organization Sea Web, pollock is also one of the safest, cleanest seafood choices out there for kids. It's also considered sustainable by the Marine Stewardship Council, the global certifier of sustainable wild fish. Maybe fish sticks are the answer to step 6 of our family-friendly meal makeover: seafood.

But before loading up our grocery cart, we remember that these are *fish sticks* we're talking about — in other words, high in fat, sodium, and additives, unless they're "natural," in which case they're just high in fat and sodium. To gum up the works more, Environmental Defense, an environmental advocacy organization, writes on its Web site that "although [the Pacific pollock] fishery is well managed, some experts are concerned that the fishery reduces the amount of food available to endangered Steller sea lions."

Sea lions?

That's all right. Fish sticks wouldn't have worked anyway, because three of the four of us absolutely love fresh, local seafood;

after all, we do live in New England. As Jean Kerr writes in her book *Mystic Seafood,* "The New England experience — and our history — has everything to do with the ocean and the bounty that comes from it." Zack, Andy, and I couldn't agree more, and as a way to celebrate this unique heritage, we even did a real, old-fashioned clambake by the sea one summer. The end result was raw lobster and mushy clams, but the sun, sand, history, and romance made it all worthwhile.

Of course, lobster and clams are just some of the wonderful options available to us; as the book points out, our waters are filled with an embarrassment of edible riches — bivalves, fin fish, and crustaceans of all sorts — but of all the choices listed, there's nothing more quintessentially New England than firm fleshed, mild white cod. As the author puts it, "When you eat a piece of cod, you are taking a bite out of New England history."

So one night when we're out for dinner, feeling inspired and in touch with our storied past, I order cod cakes. But while they're perfectly crispy, there's a nagging voice in the back of my head saying that something isn't quite right. When we get home I race to the computer, only to find Atlantic cod on every single environmental Web site under sections labeled Avoid or Worst Choice, or color-coded red. From Oceans Alive: "U.S. and Canadian stocks remain extremely depleted. Poor management and unreported catches threaten its recovery. Atlantic cod are caught with bottom trawls, which damage bottom habitat and result in considerable bycatch." Or as George Leonard, senior science manager at the world renowned Monterey Bay Aquarium's Seafood Watch program, says, "New England groundfish fisheries are in dire straits right now. It's looking catastrophic."

I immediately regret that dinner, but what should I have eaten instead? I have no idea. Meanwhile, my cynical inner teenager can't help noticing that these environmental advocacy groups say we should be boycotting the fresh stuff from Gloucester, a mere forty minutes away, but that it's okay to buy frozen cod shipped in from Alaska. And then I notice that of the twenty northeast Atlantic fish listed in the *Mystic Seafood* table of contents, only a few are given even one thumb up by the environmental groups: clams, mackerel, bass, scallops, and lobster (thank God).

JUST THE FACTS

In October 2006 the Institute of Medicine issued a report called "Seafood Choices: Balancing Benefits and Risks" that concluded, "The committee determined that no easy equation adequately expresses the complexity of the benefit and risk trade-offs involved in making seafood choices." For this "conclusion" we need an international panel of experts? Buying seafood has turned into a creepy game show. What's behind door number one: toxins, depleted species, or a delicious lobster stew?

We're tired of not knowing what to make for dinner; we also wonder if by any small chance we might be unintentionally poisoning Zack with our so-called healthy meals. The kid simply loves seafood. I took him out for a special mom–son bonding dinner before he left on a three-night school trip. We'd never been apart for that long, and we were feeling both celebratory and a little misty. Knowing what we were about to learn would probably turn us off to certain fish forever, I ordered the tuna tartare. The gleaming fresh fish was perfectly complemented by sesame oil, creamy avocado puree, and crispy wonton crackers. Not surprisingly, Zack loved it and proceeded to eat half my order.

As soon as we were done, I couldn't help wondering how much I'd damaged my beloved child with that appetizer. The time had come to wrestle the seafood alligator to the ground. We already knew that fish often contain methylmercury, PCBs, and dioxin, but we figured it couldn't be as bad as everyone says. The amount of pollutants in fish has to be infinitesimal, right?

So we decided to push forward with step 6 by researching toxins in seafood. Here's what the Centers for Disease Control and Prevention (CDC) has to say about mercury: "Exposure to high levels of mercury can cause neurologic and kidney disorders," and "exposure of childbearing-aged women is of particular concern because of the potential adverse neurologic effects of mercury in fetuses."

Kidney disorders? Neurologic effects in fetuses?

The Natural Resources Defense Council adds that "mercury actually concentrates in the umbilical cord blood that goes to the fetus, so mercury levels as low as 3.4 micrograms per liter of a mother's blood are now a concern. Nearly one in 10 women of reproductive age in the United States has mercury in her blood at or above this level, according to the CDC." I'm desperately trying to remember what I ate when I was pregnant with Zack and Maya. I have no idea. Then I read that the EPA says a study on children ages four to eight found that those with higher fish consumption had "significantly higher" levels of mercury in their urine. I really regret that tuna tartare appetizer.

As for PCBs, a panel of the European Food Safety Authority writes, "Due to their persistence in the environment, PCBs released in the past can still be found today. Non-dioxin-like (NDL) PCBs and dioxin-like-PCBs accumulate together along the food chain; they are stored in fat tissue and take a long time to leave the body. As a result, compared to fruits and vegetables, higher concentrations are found in food of animal origin, particularly in carnivores and predatory fish." Ninety percent of human exposure to NDL PCBs comes through food. And while no one's really clear on the effect of these bad boys on human health, it's probably not positive. Forget fish for a minute. If we needed yet another reason to eat less meat, we seem to have found it.

As I'm doing all this reading, I realize how glad I am that Andy packed the kids' lunches this morning, because at this point, I'm not sure what I'd have put in there. Filtered water and organic apples? I'm starting to think I know too much, and I haven't even gotten to dioxin yet. According to the National Institute of Environmental Health Sciences, "Studies have shown that dioxin exposure at high levels in exposed chemical workers leads to an increase in cancer. Other studies in highly exposed people show that dioxin exposure can lead to reproductive and developmental problems, increased heart disease and increased diabetes." And though they also write that "the effect of the long term low level exposure that is normally experienced by the general population is not known," we'd rather not experiment on our children.

Data collection is chipping away at our buoyancy. And our appetites.

Then we hear of a study published in the journal *Science* warning that if we don't implement worldwide conservation efforts soon, the world's wild-caught seafood fisheries could collapse by 2050. "Marine biodiversity loss is increasingly impairing the ocean's capacity to provide food, maintain water quality, and recover from perturbations," the report concluded.

Our heads are already hanging low, so we shouldn't be surprised when we come across the statement that in addition to being unclean and unsustainable, eating fish is also *unethical*. This comes from *The Way We Eat* by Peter Singer and Jim Mason, although they do make an exception for bivalves, including oysters, clams, and scallops. On the bright side, as long as they've been farmed, these three are also pretty low in toxins. Of course, neither Andy nor Maya will eat them, although Andy will eat scallops, preferably wrapped in bacon. So if we want our seafood dinners to be relatively low in toxins, sustainable, safe for children to eat and not harmful to sentient beings, in our house we will be able to eat expensive and hard-to-find farmed bay scallops and that's pretty much it.

DIZZY

When we started this makeover, one of our goals was to get Maya to eat at least one bite of non-ikura fish. But after learning how polluted and endangered seafood is, and in some eyes also immoral, we wonder, *why* did we want her to again? Oh yeah, nutritionists say we should be eating it twice a week because it's high in protein and beneficial omega-3 fatty acids and low in saturated fat. Not to mention, certain fish and shellfish are high in *iron* and *zinc*.

We're ready to give up on seafood and move right on to step 7 — snacks — when I come across another, more upbeat report. A clinical review by doctors at the Harvard School of Public Health, published in October 2006 in the *Journal of the American Medical Association,* states unequivocally that when it comes to fish consumption, "It is striking how much greater both the amount of evidence and the size of the health effect are for health benefits, compared with health risks."

Now we're getting somewhere. Break out the tuna tartare! Then again, we realize that the authors of this study weren't focusing on kids, so we take special note from Seafood Watch on toxins: "The most vulnerable populations are children and women who are pregnant or are thinking of becoming pregnant."

The Harvard clinical review: "Levels of PCBs and dioxin in fish are low, similar to those in several other foods, and the magnitudes of possible risks in adults are greatly exceeded by benefits of fish intake."

KidSafe Seafood: "Fish are a nutritious source of lean protein, vitamins, minerals, and omega-3 fatty acids. Even so, parents of growing children — just like pregnant moms — need to be aware that some fish contain toxic pollutants harmful to kids."

If this were a tennis match, our heads would have fallen off by now: back, forth, back, forth, it's safe, it's not, it's SAFE, it's NOT . . . I'm on the phone talking all this over with Tim Fitzgerald, a scientist with the Oceans Program at Environmental Defense in New York, and I start laughing skittishly. Maya is in the other room with a fever she's had for six days. The first nor'easter of the year has just hit and Andy can't get the snowblower to start. Zack is bored, and that's never good. The toilet is clogged and swear to God, try as I might, I can't get the plunger to work — Andy? And in the midst of all this domestic chaos, we're supposed to finagle our way through a hellish quagmire of conflicting information and come out the other side still eating fish and maybe even smiling too?

In the blink of an eye, seafood has turned into the rabbit hole, which "went straight on like a tunnel for some way, and then dipped suddenly down, so suddenly that Alice had not a moment to think about stopping herself before she found herself falling down a very deep well."

Are you there, God? It's me, Alice. I've fallen and I can't get up.

OMEG-HUH?

This would all be a moot point — Zack could load up on grass-fed burgers and Maya would happily subsist only on pasta — but for three things: (1) we live in a seafood mecca, (2) 75 percent of us love seafood, and (3) omega-3 fatty acids.

Fatty acids are where things fall apart even more. The science is just plain confusing, at least to laymen like us, and while there are charts and graphs and all sorts of visual aids meant to clarify things, none of it is enough. Fatty acids quickly devolve into a blur of letters: LA, ALA, DHA, EPA — isn't that last one the government agency that always disagrees with the FDA?

Just when I'm up to my elbows in omega-3s, I hear, "Hey, Mom?" That's Zack calling from the other room. He's sick today, which means that twelve out of the past fourteen weekdays, at least one kid has stayed home because of illness, snow, or school vacation. Plus, while Roxy has basically made a full recovery from her stroke, for which we're very grateful, she's also gone a little senile, barking pretty much all the time; she just stands in the living room and barks, barks, barks.

Before losing heart and quitting the meal makeover for good, we decide to cut our losses and cut to the chase, which is simply this: fish rich in omega-3 fatty acids seem to be great for overall health. (We know this is waffly, imprecise language, but in this instance we're following the lead of brilliant PhDs the world over. Besides, how something called "fatty acids" can be good for you is beyond us in the first place.) Omega-3s are said to help prevent coronary heart disease, and some researchers are looking into claims they can reduce inflammation and act as a mood enhancer.

Anything to help with our collectively dismal midwinter mood sounds good, and while we're at it both Andy and I, along with most of our middle-aged friends, suffer from joint pain. But now that we know how contaminated most seafood is, we wonder whether we can just get those omega-3s from other, cleaner sources. After all, vitamins and minerals are available in all sorts of foods (and supplements, which have pretty much turned into a lost cause with Zack, but which still remain a tantalizing possibility nonetheless) — can't we just avoid fish altogether? What about walnuts and flaxseed? What about purified fish oil supplements? *What about omega-3-rich algae supplements?* If any of these worked, then we could bypass fish altogether. Even better, we could just eat vitamin- and omega-3 fortified cookies, which should be on the market any day now. That would make the kids happy.

Without getting back into incomprehensible strings of letters, the short answer is, so unfairly, no. Except for the carcinogenic, memory-killing, tremor-causing toxic chemicals they contain, fish are just plain good for you. Most experts agree there are at least some health benefits to be derived from ingesting long-chain fatty acids (i.e., omega-3s from seafood), and since our bodies can't make them, we have to get them from our diets.

Because this is fish we're talking about, though, it's still not clear whether the main health effects derive from its inherent goodness or rather because a meal of tilapia displaces one of, say, maple-ginger glazed pork ribs. (So it better be tasty tilapia is all we can say.) Indeed, at the end of the Institute of Medicine report, the authors conclude that "an organization of experts is needed among appropriate federal agencies to oversee and manage coordinated benefit–risk judgments and to implement a coordinated research effort to generate the data needed by agencies to issue timely, accurate, and continuously updated advice to consumers." They're not even kidding. But while we may need advisories, we're not getting any yet; in the meantime, there's still dinner to make.

Ultimately we've come to understand that despite all the disadvantages, it's probably worthwhile to serve seafood to the kids. Fine, but that still begs the question of which fish to serve — a question we'll have to answer for ourselves, at least until our dream team of inter-agency experts is putting out clear, decisive, weekly advisories in grocery stores.

Still, Andy's not worried. "It's not like we're eating fish every day," he says calmly. He's on the road for work, checking in on his cell.

"But we would be!" I exclaim.

"Fish is inconvenient," he says laconically on the other end of the phone. "You have to buy it the same day you eat it."

"This is depressing!" I reply.

"What am I gonna do?" he asks irritably, now provoked. "Shoot myself? Everything we're finding out is horrible. It's not a fun way to live. Listen, I'm near Lionette's. Whaddya want?"

"Maybe we should have hamburgers for dinner."

THE FUTURE OF FISH

In September 2006 the Food and Agriculture Organization of the United Nations reported that nearly half the fish eaten as food worldwide is farmed rather than caught in the wild. And while many people turn up their noses at farmed fish, we're fine with it, especially if it means we can keep feeding the kids seafood. Or rather, feeding Zack, and trying to tempt Maya.

If we're looking at aquaculture, though, we have to talk about salmon, one of the most commonly eaten fish in the United States.

Seafood Watch (and many others) has this to say about farmed salmon (also called "Atlantic salmon," or "ocean-farmed salmon," and sometimes even erroneously labeled — and priced — as much more expensive wild salmon): "Many farmed fish, including most farmed salmon, are raised in net pens, like cattle in a feedlot."

Now that we know more about feedlots? Gross.

"Thousands of fish concentrated in one area produce tons of feces, polluting the water. Diseases can spread from fish in the crowded pens to wild fish. Antibiotics and other drugs used to control those diseases leak out into the environment, creating drug-resistant disease organisms. And if farmed fish escape their pens, they can take over habitat from wild fish in the area." One final point: farmed salmon are also fed colorants to make them pink so they'll look, well, like salmon.

But it's so cheap and tasty that we'd love for all this to be wrong, so hoping to uncover some rare good news we head over to the Web site for industry group Salmon of the Americas. It says that environmental assessments, "when done with unbiased scientific scrutiny, consistently find that salmon farming poses a low risk to the environment, and the impacts that do occur are fully reversible through natural processes in a relatively short period of time."

I'm ready to make a beeline for the store, but then both Andy and I remember hearing about sea lice, a parasite found in farmed salmon that infects juvenile wild salmon populations. I write to Salmon of the Americas and ask about the farmed salmon–sea lice connection; they never write back. We take this as a bad sign.

How about organic farmed fish? That seems to cover all the bases, but then Tim Fitzgerald from Environmental Defense warns in an e-mail, "There are organically-certified fish available for sale in the U.S. These are largely certified by private agencies in Europe (e.g., Naturland or the Soil Association), but the standards vary across certifiers and across species. Some are better than others, but the USDA does not offer reciprocity for any of them since it doesn't have standards of its own." Bottom line: he doesn't recommend buying organic seafood until the USDA is onboard.

Hoping three's a charm, I contact George Leonard again. He has kids too, so he understands what we're up against here. Could he please direct us to a safe, clean farmed fish that not only tastes good but is also high in omega-3 fatty acids? This would seem like a fool's errand, but he comes right back at me with the name of a company called Australis and it's in western Massachusetts, just an hour and a half away. So in addition to everything else, it's also local, at least sort of, since while the fingerlings were originally flown in from Australia, these days they're mostly hatched onsite.

Once again, I have it in my head that we can take the kids on an educational field trip, but by now everyone's onto my ways, so this type of discussion has gotten really short.

"Hey," I say enthusiastically one night over a hopefully mostly mercury-, PCB- and dioxin-free family dinner of bean and cheese tacos, "there's this really cool fish farm a couple hours away from here. Do either of you want to go?"

"A *fish farm*?" Zack says snidely. "What's a *fish farm*?"

Maya: "NO!"

"Actually," Zack says, "I don't want to go either. I'd rather go to school, if you can believe it." I look across at Andy, and he looks back at me.

"Do you want to go?" I ask him in a small voice.

"Sure, I'll go."

"Because you want to, or because you're doing it for me?"

"A little of both," he admits. So that's how a couple weeks later Andy and I find ourselves once again dropping the kids off at school while we head out to western Massachusetts, to see our very first fish farm.

Managing Director Josh Goldman has been involved with aquaculture for two decades; now he's working with barramundi, an Australian white fish that's low in fat and relatively high in omega-3 fatty acids, as well as free of hormones, antibiotics, colorants, and mercury. Australis uses a closed-containment system, so the fish can't escape and affect wild species (like some other farmed fish we know); almost all the water is filtered and recycled, and the little that's left over exceeds EPA standards for cleanliness. The Australis system uses less fish meal and more vegetarian feed than some other farmed fish, so barramundi is less contaminated and uses fewer resources; and finally, the fish manure is used as fertilizer by local farmers.

The fish sounds perfect in every way, although the farm itself is nothing to get excited about; it's a series of gigantic tanks containing thousands of fish set in warehouse-style rooms with wet, slippery floors. Australis wouldn't have done much for Zack, and Maya would've made us pay if we'd brought her. (To us it doesn't smell fishy, but to her it probably would have been nasal torture.) Even I'm glad they didn't come. I may finally be learning a lesson here: unless proven otherwise, the kids would rather stay home. Food for thought. Anyway, with its environmental and health pedigrees, Australis barramundi is obviously angling to become the celebrity fish of the decade. Seafood Watch has even added it to the site's Best Choices list.

The day after we go to Australis, Andy gets lab results back from his most recent annual physical. His doctor has circled some number on the page and written, "You are on the edge of diabetes. Let's repeat this test in 3 months. Don't panic though." Andy panics, in his own, understated way; that is to say, he gets mad. He's already taking cholesterol medication, albeit erratically. In his opinion, this shouldn't be happening to him.

Suddenly we're glad there's a clinical review on fish intake and human health written by two Harvard doctors whose focus is heart disease sitting on the desk, and while they say that the evidence is "inconclusive" and "more studies need to be done," Andy's not only switching medicines (he needs something he only has to remember once a day), he's also going on fish oil pills (and coenzyme Q10, which his doctor recommended), effective immediately.

Now there's even more reason to be eager about omega-3 rich barramundi except — small detail — we haven't tasted it yet. Whole Foods says it'll order some for us but then never does. We find out it's supposedly sold at Captain Marden's, a top-notch seafood purveyor in Wellesley, Massachusetts, but it's not in the case when Andy checks. Not wanting to come home empty-handed, he buys farmed catfish instead.

Andy, enthusiastically: "Maybe I can make catfish fingers to see if Maya will try them." I check the KidSafe Web site to make sure it's on the approved list. It's not. But as a small ray of light in an ever-darkening sky, Andy tells me that when he bought the catfish at Captain Marden's, he also special-ordered two pounds of barramundi; the guy behind the counter told him that they'd had it in the week before, but no one bought it.

The next day, Andy picks up two whole, cleaned fish and we print out a recipe from the Australis Web site for steamed barramundi Chinese-style. While he was in the store, he told me later, another customer had asked, "What's barramundi? I've never heard of it," as she paid for her swordfish. As he rushed out the door, he answered over his shoulder, "It's high in omega-3s, clean, and sustainable. You should try it." But, he adds, "I didn't tell her about the swordfish because that would have been too, you know . . ." I do know. Now that we're becoming lay experts on seafood, we both want to spread the word, but neither of us wants to turn into a zealot.

That night, the three of us share a delicious meal of sweet, white, on-the-bone barramundi in a ginger-soy-sesame sauce. (Maya has white pasta.) It's fragrant and salty and packed with flavor. Andy picks off pieces and gives them to Zack, I do the same for Andy — this is so good for his heart — and we each talk about the best parts of our day. Barramundi has turned this dinnertime into a little slice of heaven.

Is it too good to be true? Nah, there's always at least a little trouble in paradise; this time, it comes in the form of feed laced with soy, a crop that, unless it's been grown organically, has most likely been genetically modified (GM). Of course, because there's no labeling of GM foods in this country, and because soy is a major GM crop, this is probably true of almost all farmed fish, at least at this point.

But in what's looking more and more like a contaminated food supply within a contaminated world, Australis barramundi comes off smelling like a rose, so to speak. We're definitely adding it to our menu — as long as Andy happens to be going to Wellesley for work, that is, and as long as we remember to preorder it.

In other words, we still haven't found the golden key that will unlock the mysteries of seafood.

THE ANSWER, AT LEAST FOR NOW

Since not even organic farmed salmon or barramundi can dig us out of this fishy hole, and realizing that the average Jane can't make heads or tails of all this business, a handful of organizations have compiled lists of which fish are safe, or sustainable, or safe *and* sustainable to eat. Once in a while Andy or I will see one and clip it out, but then, feeling overwhelmed, we'll forget about it again. Case in point: the lime green sticky on the desk right now. It keeps getting buried under papers, then reappears when one of us cleans up. This is what's written on it in a messy scrawl:

Shrimp
Canned light tuna
Salmon
Pollock
Catfish

Neither of us can remember where this list originated — we think it was a magazine, we're not sure — but it was definitely touted as a guide to "good" seafood options. But what did "good" mean? It's hard to know, especially when we look it over now and see that "salmon" doesn't differentiate between farmed and wild, shrimp is its own can of worms, and canned tuna is a veritable volcano ready to blow. Meanwhile, shrimp, canned tuna, and farmed salmon have been some of the most commonly eaten seafood in this country since 1991.

So I throw that sticky in the trash and head over to the Web site of the highly reputable Monterey Bay Aquarium's Seafood Watch program. It has regional lists organized into three color-coded sections: green, or Best Choices; yellow, or Good Alternatives; and red, or Avoid. Then there are red stars by some of the fish, even those in the green column, which denote high mercury content, and blue stars by some fish, which means those selections are certified as sustainable by the Marine Stewardship Council — but that doesn't always mean they're *clean*. Even if we could unravel the complexities of the list, we wonder if all this is applicable to kids too.

I call George Leonard of Seafood Watch again. "Seafood makes meat seem like a cakewalk," I say with a nervous laugh; I'm trying to ease my way into the topic, because it's more than a little embarrassing that the card Seafood Watch has created specifically to simplify seafood *hasn't*, at least not for us. For example, on the Northeast guide, tuna is broken down into *eleven kinds* — skipjack and yellowfin and albacore, longline and troll/poll — just researching and memorizing tuna *alone* could take a month. We want a simpler cheat sheet.

George is kind and understanding, and he loads me up with referrals to organizations that can further confuse — that is, educate — us. For example, Environmental Defense has its own list that's a bit easier to read and sort out; the only thing is, we don't like what we see, because it turns out that if it's omega-3s we're after, then we should be eating more anchovies, Atlantic herring, Atlantic mackerel, farmed oysters, and sardines. Zack would probably be into a lot of this — oily, strong bluefish is one of his favorites (although now we've learned he shouldn't be eating that either — mercury, PCBs, and pesticides, according to Environmental Defense) — but Andy and Maya? Maya has the schnozz of a drug-sniffing dog, and cooking any one of these would make for an unpleasant evening in the house. And Andy? Maybe if we fried some of them, but otherwise, *non*.

George then sends us over to KidSafe Seafood at the Sea Web site. This list is simple all right — too simple. According to it, as of this writing, the only reliably safe seafood choices for children are:

Wild Alaskan salmon (Chum, Coho, and Pink)
Tilapia (U.S./Central American)
Farmed blue mussels
Northern U.S. and Canadian shrimp
US farmed crayfish
Farmed bay scallops

C'est tout. When, in growing despondency, I hit the "What about Other Kinds of Fish" button, we get the most overwhelming list of all telling us that Zack has been eating far too much crab and lobster (along with bluefish).

Just after learning about the extremely limited KidSafe fish list, Zack turns eleven. This year, instead of going to the East Coast Grill where the kids gorged themselves on all manner of grilled pork (including that spicy rib we all remember so fondly), the four of us, along with meat-loving Michael, are going out for seafood instead.

We get to the restaurant and realize we don't have a fish list with us. We aren't being willful. It's just that by this point we are totally bewildered about which list to use; whether PCBs are an overblown health scare or something to take seriously; which to care about most — mercury, PCBs, dioxin, or omega-3s; and whether or not our family's personal dinner choices make one iota of difference to wild fisheries worldwide.

After examining the menu with the mental equivalent of a magnifying glass I order the wood-grilled Arctic char, because it tastes great and I remember that Tim from Environmental Defense had said it's a pretty good alternative to farmed salmon. Maya always orders alphabet soup at this restaurant, and while in the past this lack of adventurousness has bothered us, today we see it as an advantage. Zack, in his Zack-ish way, orders crispy smelts and eats them bone and all. And Michael, when he hears that I, like his mom, won't let him get swordfish, asks if he can have scallops instead. The KidSafe list says that farm-raised scallops from somewhere — around here? — are fine, but the chalkboard doesn't say whether these are farm raised or wild. I don't have it in me to get into all of it with the server, so I tell Michael that yes, he can have scallops, and keep my fingers crossed that even if they're not KidSafe approved, then at least they're not *too* terrible.

I look across the table at Andy. "What are you having?"

He raises his eyebrows in reply.

"Sword?" I venture. He nods. I smile and say nothing; for just this meal, the health of the seas will have to wait. It's hard, though, because Andy thinks this is just a mercury issue. Ultimately, of course, I'll have to break the news to him, and since patience isn't my strong suit, I wait for all of a day, until just the two of us are in the car, before casually asking, "Did you know that swordfish isn't just a mercury issue but that it's also overfished?"

"No."

"If you knew that, would you order it? I'm just curious." (Such a lie. This is obviously a test and we both know it.)

Andy shakes his head. "That'd be tough." Swordfish is by far his favorite fish. "I'm just a squirrel trying to get a nut," he says, almost pleadingly. He's beaten down. By life. By fish.

We want to make good choices we can all live with and not feel deprived, but after scanning all the lists out there, we realize none of them quite meets our needs. We're too busy for yellow sections, multicolored asterisks or asides in tiny print. Instead, after collating, cross-pollinating, and consulting with experts from New

York to California, I come up with Everymom's Middle-of-the-Road Fish List. It's obviously imperfect; after all, even the experts can't agree, the recommendations will change over time, and it's oversimplified in some cases. But at least it's an attempt to take a first step back to eating seafood with a semblance of confidence after a month of fish madness.

EVERYMOM'S MIDDLE-OF-THE-ROAD FISH LIST

Green
Wild-caught salmon from Alaska (fresh, frozen, or
    canned)
Barramundi (U.S. farmed; *not* Nile perch, a problematic
    invasive species, which is sometimes mislabeled as
    barramundi)
Sardines
Anchovies
Atlantic herring
Atlantic mackerel (*not* king or Spanish)
Oysters (farmed)
Arctic char
Bay scallops (farmed)
Tilapia (U.S. farmed)
Mussels (farmed)
Tiny salad shrimp
Crayfish (U.S. farmed; have never seen them at the store in
    Boston)
Catfish (U.S. farmed)
Clams (farmed)
Crab (*not* king crab from Russia)

Pacific cod (*not* Atlantic cod)
Calamari/squid
Wild-caught pollock from Alaska
Anything from Henry & Lisa's Natural Seafood brand
    (www.ecofish.com)

NB: Canned tuna is a conundrum. If pregnant women or children
are eating it a couple times a week or even once a week, it's worth
buying the kind that's been tested for mercury — look for Ecofish,
Wild Planet, Dave's Albacore, or any other brand that says it's tested
low for mercury. Not up for thinking about it? Just replace it with
canned wild salmon (go for boneless/skinless, otherwise it looks a
little scary when you open the can).

Red
Tilapia from China and Taiwan
Chilean seabass/toothfish
Atlantic cod
Atlantic flounder, sole, haddock, hake, halibut
Monkfish
Orange roughy
Farmed salmon (aka Atlantic salmon, ocean-farmed
    salmon)
Shark
Skate
Red snapper
Grouper
Imported caviar
Swordfish
American tuna
Tilefish

Top Seven Clean, Omega-3-Rich Fish

1. Wild-caught salmon from Alaska (fresh, frozen, or canned)
2. Barramundi (U.S. farmed; *not* Nile perch, a problematic invasive species, which is sometimes mislabeled as barramundi)
3. Sardines
4. Anchovies
5. Atlantic herring
6. Atlantic mackerel (*not* king or Spanish)
7. Oysters (farmed)

To find out about fish oil supplements, go to www .oceansalive.org and click on Eat Smart. (For more fishy information, see appendix.)

A SOMEWHAT HAPPY ENDING TO THE FISH TALE

Back at the beginning of this whole seafood farce, long before we'd come up with our own fish list, I'd asked Tim from Environmental Defense whether our purchases actually matter. I was just thinking that this is all so tiring, and tiresome, and we'd really like to forget we ever brought the issue up so we could go back to being dumb, uninformed consumers of fantastically good tuna tartare. He said our purchases do matter, "a lot."

Seriously? I pushed him. You're not just saying that to make us feel better or guiltier or something? "Individual purchasing power is extremely important," he said. "As my boss says, go to the supermarket and try to buy "dolphin-unsafe" tuna — consumers basically changed the way tuna are caught." Then I remember that the 2006 report in *Science* warning of the imminent collapse of wild

Fish Tips

According to Environmental Defense, try the following tips to reduce levels of PCBs, dioxins, and some pesticides in fish:

- Before cooking, remove the skin, fat (found along the back, sides, and belly), internal organs, tomalley of lobster, and the mustard of crabs, where toxins are likely to accumulate. This will greatly reduce the risk of exposure to a number of hazardous chemicals.

- When cooking, let the fat drain away, and avoid or reduce fish drippings.

- Serve less fried fish. Frying seals in chemical pollutants that might be in the fish's fat, whereas grilling, broiling, or poaching allows fat to drain away.

- For smoked fish, it is best to fillet the fish and remove the skin before the fish is smoked.

fisheries had gone on to say, "Available data suggest that at this point, these trends are still reversible."

Though the tuna and swordfish and bluefish (and on and on) lovers in us will never quite get over the loss, we see that we have a job to do, and that as long as we're conscientious shoppers, we can still be an omega-3-rich, happy, healthy, seafood-eating family. Once again we're filled with cautious optimism. It had been a while. And while implementing step 6 definitely takes some extra work, we seem to have made it through the worst of it and come out the other side. If we can find our way through the morass that is seafood, we can surely handle anything else this woolly meal makeover might have in store for us.

Chapter 5 ½

. . . .

At the Table: Take 4

Tonight we're feeling on top of our game: we're serving fish chowder featuring two Green choices. This sounds great as long as you overlook that the cod is shipped in from Alaska. Then there's the crab to consider. A few minutes ago when we were about to start cooking I pulled the container Andy had bought from the fridge and read the label: "Wild swimming blue," it said, and "Product of Thailand." Our homemade list doesn't mention this type, and neither does our wallet-sized version, so I go into my office to look it up. The Seafood Watch Web site lists thirteen types of crab, and while none of them match up with what we have, I have a sinking suspicion this is actually blue king crab from Russia, which is under the Avoid category owing to poor management.

I always feel like such a schmuck at times like this — who wants to be the bearer of bad news all the time? — and if Andy and I weren't married, I'd have thanked him for shopping and left it at that. "Best-laid plans," he mutters when I tell him, and "Backed into a corner," then glumly, "Lord knows I try." I feel for him, I really do, and obviously I want the wild Thai crab to be fine, too. But whether it is or isn't, it's already in the house and it's dinnertime, so it's getting turned into soup. On this, we both agree.

"Can I help cook?" Maya asks enthusiastically when she sees us cutting celery. "I love to cook!"

"Will you eat it if you cook it?"

"Uh, I don't *think* so." We figured this would be her answer, but every once in a while we come across another article saying that when kids help cook or garden or shop, they're much more willing to eat whatever they helped grow or prepare. This tactic has rarely worked in our house, but one of us tries it out from time to time, if only to prove to ourselves that we're putting our best foot forward. Instead she heads into the other room to find Zack.

When the chowder's done, the kids come into the kitchen to wash their hands.

"Pee-yew, that soup smells *bad,*" Maya exclaims.

"Will you try it?" I foolishly ask.

"*No,*" she yells. Then she starts crying. After she's pulled herself together, she sees the little bowl of bacon bits I've set aside for sprinkling on top of the chowder and sweetly asks, "Mama, can I have some of the bacon plain since I don't like the soup?"

Wow, I think; this girl really knows how to kick a mom when she's down. I reluctantly say yes, but hoping she'll forget, I hide the bowl behind a flower vase. My ploy works, because she doesn't mention bacon again for the rest of the night.

For dinner Maya has consented to (local, leftover) hamburger, peas, olives, and whole wheat bread. Earlier, Zack had said he wasn't in the mood for soup, but now that there's a big steaming bowl in front of him, he wolfs it down. Andy does the same. And while I think the cod is delicious, the crab tastes sort of, I don't know, overfished. I can't eat it. Andy looks over at my mostly full bowl. "I didn't know what do," he explains defensively. "I asked if they had local crab at the store, but they didn't."

"No problem," I respond kindly. "But next time, maybe we should leave the crab out."

He nods.

"We'll figure it all out someday," I say reassuringly. As we've learned, having a fish list and using it are two entirely different matters. Still, while progress may be coming in fits and starts, we're doing our best.

Chapter 6

. . . .

The Vexing People Problem

MARKETING MADNESS

"P"lease, Mommy? Please?" Maya's holding on to my leg and looking up at me with wide, urgent eyes, imploring me to get her a snack. She's trying to be irresistible, and it's almost working. Almost, but not quite.

We're at the health club because Maya recently asked if she could take swimming lessons, so every Tuesday after school the two of us head over to the indoor pool. This is great because since it was her idea, she's more likely to learn how to swim and she gets much-needed exercise during the winter. It's a win-win any way you look at it — except for one small detail: on our way in and out of the building, we pass by a snack machine.

The first time I see it, in an effort to block Maya's view, I quickly maneuver things so that I'm between her and the dreaded machine as we walk through the room. My tactic doesn't work. She peers around me and spies it; from that day forward my sweet, impressionable daughter begins to beg, whine, and generally bug the crap out of me every time we go to swim lessons.

The main entryway to the building isn't the only place we encounter obstacles to healthy eating at the "health club," because this pool is where we also met GooGoo Cluster supplier, Paige. When the two of us are getting our kids dressed after a lesson one day, Paige pulls out some snack options from her designer bag ("low-end," she clarifies) that look much more appealing than anything I have to offer. There are Cheez-Its or crackers on her side of the room, versus a soy nut butter sandwich or cut-up carrots on mine — if I've remembered to bring anything at all for Maya, that is. While I keep saying I want to change, for years I've been a terrible mooch at playgrounds, parks, and apparently now even locker rooms all over greater Boston. Anyway, when Paige sees what I've brought she laughingly shakes her head and wags her finger at me. Next she notices Maya looking wistfully in her direction, then graciously offers some of whatever she has.

But even Paige avoids the machine in the front hallway, and she recently told me about a door that goes directly to the pool, therefore bypassing it altogether. I thanked her profusely, figuring that if Maya didn't see the machine, over time she'd forget about it. I was wrong. These days the whining sometimes starts *before* we get in the car to drive to the pool. Finally worn down, one day I tell her that at the end of her eight-week session she can have a treat. From then on that, instead of swimming, becomes her focus: how many weeks left until her treat, how many can she get, could it be sweet . . .

With every subject we tackle — vitamin and mineral deficiency in children, factory-farmed meat, unfair trade, the seafood nightmare — Andy and I think we've come to the most challenging topic of all. But as the makeover train pulls up to stop 7, the Snack Station, we discover with a shudder that this one might take the prize. That's because snacks, which are a daily (and sometimes even hourly) part of life with kids, are really about the willful, and sadly successful, attempt by corporations to turn a profit, regardless of the impact on children's health.

Kelly D. Brownell, PhD, cofounder and director of the Rudd

Center for Food Policy and Obesity at Yale, writes in a 2006 World Health Organization (WHO) report:

> The marketing of food to children accomplishes what industry intends. Cultivated as consumers at very early ages, children are trained to desire foods and beverages whose typical consumption may compromise health. Science on the topic is abundant and converges on unambiguous conclusions, namely that such marketing to children increases:
>
> - consumption
> - preference for energy-dense, low-nutrient foods and beverages
> - purchase requests
> - purchases
> - positive beliefs about food and beverage products

As the Rudd Center Web site explains, "Using war-like terms to describe their new methods (guerilla marketing, viral marketing, stealth marketing), the industry markets aggressively in magazines, over the Internet, in schools, with product placements in movies and subsequent tie-ins with food products and fast food chains, and much more . . . The ability of parents to shield their children from marketing has been low for years and is now eroded further."

CONSUMING KIDS

Wanting to know more about how marketers work, I contact Susan Linn, EdD, the author of *Consuming Kids* and cofounder of the advocacy group Campaign for a Commercial-Free Childhood. As both a psychologist and a nationally known expert on marketing to children, she's the perfect person to talk to; she's even right here in Boston. We set up a time for an interview at her downtown office. Better still, Maya gets invited on a playdate that same afternoon, and Andy can take Zack to his office. Sometimes, the universe provides.

Except the universe must not be a mom, because It seemed to forget that while Maya has recently grown comfortable enough to do a drop-off playdate, she won't actually let this other mom, Cathy, take her home from school. The night before the play-date, Maya tearfully reminds us of her need to be escorted to the friend's house. So if I want her to be able to play with her friend, and if I don't want to inconvenience everyone by canceling at the last minute, I will have to downgrade my meeting with this hero to a phone interview so I can pick Maya up and take her to this other family's house, literally a two-minute walk from school.

It's not ideal, but at least we're all set — that is, until Cathy calls while the girls are at school to tell me her two-year-old has just thrown up. Playdate canceled. I make alternative child-care ar-rangements with Stacia; just as I get off the phone with her, Cathy calls again — her son is up and running around and he seems fine. It turns out that when she called the first time, she had been too embarrassed to tell me she'd fed him popcorn, which she couldn't avoid because his big brother had a friend over, and we all know how these things go. Playdate back on. I get to school to undertake the elaborate handoff ritual; that's when Maya says she's willing to go home with Cathy after all. So off they all go, Maya and her little friend hand in hand. It's lucky that I have a sense of humor. And a flexible job.

It's all worth it in the end, though, because Susan and I finally get the chance to speak. She confirms what Andy and I already suspect: it's not just us against our kids, it's us against an entire industry of adults lined up behind our kids, whispering billions of dollars' worth of sweet nothings in their ears. These marketers know that kids are perpetually hungry. They also know that children care about their snacks deeply and truly, because snacks aren't just about taste; they're also about *image*. Wear the wrong clothes, listen to the wrong music, eat the wrong food, and a kid can become the target of some unpleasant attention.

Susan says that companies actually team up with anthropologists and child psychologists "to exploit developmental vulnerabilities in children," not just by employing bright colors and TV characters but also by figuring out what matters most to kids at various ages — sensitive issues of identity and belonging and power — and then using this knowledge against them. As Andy says in a singsongy voice, "That's not ni-ice."

"Psychologists like me tell parents to pick their battles," Susan says. "But now, because commercialization is just so omnipresent, it's hard to know which battles to pick: the violent media battle? The precocious sexuality battle? It's easier to give in on food, but childhood obesity is a major public health problem." The 2006 WHO report goes further, asserting, "Poor diets and diseases related to them constitute a public health emergency."

In fact, according to a 2006 report from the Institute of Medicine, "One third of American children and youth are either obese or at risk of becoming obese. Over the past 30 years, the obesity rate has nearly tripled for children ages 2–5 years, and youth ages 12–19 years, and quadrupled for children ages 6–11 years." The CDC says that one of the government's national objectives for 2010 is "the reduction in the proportion of children and adolescents who are overweight or obese . . . However, the [most recent] overweight estimates suggest that since 1994, overweight in youths has not leveled off or decreased, and is increasing to even higher levels. The data for adolescents are of notable concern because overweight adolescents are at increased risk to become overweight adults."

"The marketers talk about 'parental responsibility' and say that parents should 'just say no,'" Susan says, and at this — I can't help myself — I laugh out loud, but then quickly add, "I don't think this is funny, it's just —"

"I know," she interjects compassionately. "Sometimes all you can do is laugh. The more I know about marketing to children, the worse it gets." She tells me that companies purposely go after kids when parents aren't around, on Web sites, kids' TV, and even in schools.

That's why, in an effort to help our kids maintain at least a semblance of a healthy diet when they're out of the house, we pack their lunches every day. In fact, a friend of Zack's once told me that he has the healthiest lunches in the entire school. Other kids get chips and cookies in their lunch boxes — or, heaven forbid, money for the cafeteria — but ours don't get any of the above. Instead their midday meals are made up of hummus and carrots, cut-up veggies, a little ham or soy nut butter, and almost always fresh fruit. Their healthy meals garner raves from teachers and even the principal, but the response among their peers isn't quite as rosy. They both get teased.

But we keep up the good fight because we know it's the right thing to do. Still, some days we can't help asking ourselves, All this and for what? As we found out when we were doing our food diary for Dr. Roberts, the kids are feasting on all sorts of illicit junk when they're at school. There are birthday cupcakes, ice-cream fund-raisers, and surreptitiously traded lunch items (not allowed, but it still happens). There's candy given out. There are school parties. It never stops. Recently while doing the laundry, I found a

chocolate wrapper crumpled up in Zack's pants pocket; meanwhile, Maya spends one afternoon a week at Andy's office hanging
around with Stacia's mom, Sue, who is also Andy's office manager
and treats our kids as if they were her own grandchildren. And
why not? It's fun to give kids what they want — especially when
you're not the one dealing with the sugar buzz afterward. Yes, yes,
Science disputes whether sugar makes kids hyper, but Science isn't
in our house after Maya's had ice cream just before bedtime.

In the end, despite all our hard work, and despite loving at least
some of the pushers, could it be that our snack makeover efforts
will all be in vain?

SICKENINGLY SWEET

I see the scope of what we're up against when I come across this
story in Marion Nestle's book, *What to Eat*: "A couple of weeks
after my book *Food Politics* came out in 2002, I received an unexpected letter from a Washington, D.C., law firm representing the
Sugar Association." The letter, she goes on, "said that in talking
about my book on a radio program, I had made 'numerous false,
misleading, disparaging, and defamatory statements about sugar,'
first among them that I 'continuously repeat the false and inaccurate statement that soft drinks contain sugar.'" She explains the
hairsplitting (and disingenuous) "science" behind the association's
claim — that sucrose qualifies as sugar but high fructose corn
syrup does not — then offers up the good news that in the end
the group never followed through on its threat to sue her.

But wait, maybe there's a silver lining at hand, because according to at least one industry representative, not everyone thinks
parents have to "just say no" all the time. Let's hear what Daniel
L. Jaffe, executive vice president of the Association of National

Advertisers, had to say in an address given to the Task Force on Media and Childhood Obesity in March of 2007. After illuminating all the ways in which the advertising industry has "proactively" addressed childhood obesity, he began his summary by saying, "We believe, however, that one key segment of society has not yet adequately stepped up to the plate in a serious and substantial way — and that is the government."

Yes, yes, yes, Mr. Jaffe! As Susan so aptly puts it in *Consuming Kids*, "As history has shown repeatedly, it's been governmental regulation, not self-regulation, that causes industry to curb exploitive practices such as child labor, sweatshops, and the dumping of toxic waste." Or as Patti Miller, vice president and director of advocacy group Children Now's Children & the Media program explained at that same March meeting, her group hopes "we can achieve more balance in the advertising of healthy versus unhealthy foods. However, if this cannot be done voluntarily, we believe Congress has an obligation to intervene on behalf of the nation's children." So well put, although, on second thought, we're not sure this is exactly where Mr. Jaffe was going with his comment.

But maybe it should be; Andy and I see the results of all those billions of dollars (ten to fifteen billion dollars for food marketing to children alone, according to many estimates) all the time, as, for example, with that health club unhealthy smack. (Oops, I meant to write *snack*. Isn't that funny. Coincidentally, *smack* is slang for heroin. Come to think of it, so is junk.)

But back to the health club. On the last day of swim class, we go into the locker room where I slowly, meticulously help Maya change back into her clothes. I'm drawing this out, chatting with Paige, generally doing anything possible to delay the moment when we'll find ourselves standing in front of that deceptively innocent machine. And while I dread this — score one for the marketing drones — in an effort to soften the blow, I try to detach and take a scientific approach. After all, Maya has been looking forward to this for so long. Will it be a letdown? Will it take her a long time to make her choice? How will she decide? I'm ready for anything, but to my surprise, as soon as we get to the front hallway, she makes her selection within seconds: Pop-Tarts.

"There were so many different snacks in there," I say casually. "Why'd you choose that one?" Of course I already know the answer: the package is bright blue, her favorite color, which someone in marketing has obviously spent billions to find out. Besides, the lettering must also speak to one of the deepest emotional needs of five-year-old girls somehow. There's probably also a drawing of Polly Pocket hidden on the label. But Maya doesn't know any of this. What's her reasoning?

"I've seen it on TV and it looked so good," she says with her mouth full. "And it is." When has she seen Pop-Tarts on TV? I thought the kids were only watching PBS. I hate it when they have their own lives right under my nose like that. Although as Susan pointed out, PBS is no haven — its characters are used in marketing rubbish to kids too. For God's sake, is nothing sacred, not even Big Bird?

Maya and I then have a discussion about Pop-Tarts, sugar, additives, fat, and advertising, because part of our makeover strategy is to get the kids to take more responsibility for themselves and their dietary choices, thereby not only reducing fights but also empowering them to make good choices for the rest of their lives à la our friend Cale's advice. Maybe if Maya knows how unhealthy Pop-Tarts are and that they won't help her grow up to be big and strong, she won't even want to have them again.

After I finish talking she says with a sigh, "I guess this will be the only Pop-Tart I have."

Sugar by Any Other Name . . .

These are all names for sweeteners: high fructose corn syrup, glucose, fructose, lactose, maltose, sucrose (white sugar), corn syrup, brown sugar, honey, malt syrup, fruit-juice concentrate, and cane sugar.

"Ever?" I ask.

"Yeah."

"Why?"

"You said it's not healthy."

That doesn't sound like someone making an empowered choice of her own.

"Well, you could have one *sometimes*," I hedge, still fruitlessly hoping she'll come around and say that, in fact, she hates Pop-Tarts.

"Like once a year?" she says hopefully. "The way I can have nail polish once a year?" Actually, I recently told her she could have it once a month after she had her nails done at a friend's house and became smitten with the whole process, but can I help it if she's still temporally challenged?

"That sounds good," I say, relieved we've come to an agreement before any tears have arrived. She eats one Pop-Tart in the car and we agree she'll save the other one for later, but thanks to a slip of the hand, it ends up in the trash.

Oh, and by the way, Maya never did learn how to swim at that health club.

Some Scary Media Facts from Commercialfreechildhood.org

- Eighty percent of TV commercials are for fast food, candy, cereal, and toys. Thirty-two percent of all ads targeted to children are for candy; 31 percent are for cereal.

- Fast-food restaurants spend three billion dollars a year on television ads aimed at children.

- On Saturday mornings, children see one food commercial about every five minutes. Most of these ads are for foods high in fat, sugar, salt, and calories.

- A preschooler's risk for obesity increases by 6 percent for every hour of TV watched per day. If there's a TV in the child's bedroom, the odds jump an additional 31 percent for every hour watched.

- Ninety-four percent of high schools, 84 percent of middle schools, and 58 percent of elementary schools allow the sale of soda or other sugar-laden drinks on their premises. The likelihood of a child becoming obese increases 1.6 times for each can of sweetened drinks consumed daily.

- Channel One, viewed in more than twelve thousand schools, regularly shows ads for soda, candy, fast food, and chips.

- Internet sites, such www.candystand.com, that allow children to play games for "free," are festooned in advertising for sugary and high-calorie snacks.

UNDER DURESS

A few days after the Pop-Tart incident, I'm upstairs taking Maya's temperature when my friend Robin leaves a message on our answering machine. (She's the one who had, simultaneously, a husband and dog with bum legs, a sick son, and her own sprained ankle.) "I have some comments to make about motherhood today," she says, followed by a curse, then followed by an apology because she realized the kids might hear her when I play the message.

As my friend Ruth says, there was only one good thing that came out of the mostly useless childbirth class we took twelve years ago: each other. Robin, Ruth, and I met while watching daunting birthing movies and doing useless breathing exercises in the claustrophobic waiting room of our midwives' office; we scooped Janet up soon after, during a postpartum exercise class. The four of us quickly became a motley family, united by the overwhelming reality of new motherhood. Over the past eleven years, we've been through a lot together — family deaths, second (and, for Ruth, third) births, health scares, and more. But while we had all the time in the world for one another when our firstborns were still young, now we're so busy with work and multiple children that we barely talk anymore. When I hear a message from one of them on our answering machine, even if it is just to voice some complaints, it's enough to make me smile. So as soon as I have a minute, I call my cursing, kvetching friend Robin back.

"My neighbor just had her first baby and I feel so *sorry* for her," she says. "She has no idea what lies ahead. Really, we should warn people." There's just a tiny touch of hysteria in her voice. "I thought I'd have a happy life with a husband, kids, and a dog, but it's *too much*." As Robin and I continue to fill each other in on the latest illnesses, work deadlines, and issues at school, not to mention *dog troubles,* we both start laughing.

But obviously, even a talk with a sympathetic friend can't make everything better. On the night she calls, Maya has had a fever for five days. Earlier in the day, the two of us had been lying on the couch together watching *Mister Rogers' Neighborhood*. At some point between lacing up his sneakers and receiving his first visitor of the day, he looked straight into the camera and sang, "I'm taking care of you." Technically he was singing to Maya and all the other little children out there watching, but for just a moment I pretended he was singing to me, and I choked up. Ah, Mr. Rogers, I thought, why'd you have to go and die?

The next night Maya's fever still hasn't broken. Indeed she seems to be getting worse. After dinner, which she didn't eat again, Zack comes over to me and whispers worriedly, "Mom, is Maya all right?" I nod with total assurance. "She's *fine*," I say, and smile lovingly at him just to prove I mean it.

But as soon as the kids are in bed, I come downstairs and break down. *Is* Maya all right? We need a relief pitcher, someone to come in and take over as parents for just a little while. We're sleep deprived; there was another huge snowstorm today; Roxy won't stop barking at the air. I have to agree with Robin — sometimes it's all too much.

This is how marketers can be so successful at brainwashing our kids — we've used up all our energy on sick family members, broken legs, and dying loved ones. And as overwhelmed as Andy and I and our friends may feel, we know that we're among the lucky ones; in *Consuming Kids,* Susan describes a 1998 report, "The Fine Art of Whining: Why Nagging Is a Kid's Best Friend," in which the industry "identifies which kinds of parents are most likely to give in to nagging. Not surprisingly, divorced parents and those with teenagers or very young children ranked highest."

Is there any way out?

SILENCE IS GOLDEN

It dawns on me one sleepless, indigestion-filled morning that by asking for snacks all the time, Zack and Maya are just doing what comes naturally; for kids, choosing their own food is one of the first ways they get a taste of autonomy. (I'd stop this inexorable march toward independence if I could, but then I'd probably have to homeschool, so — inexorable march it is.) And I admit, it's exciting to see them learn who they are and what they love most. I just wish this developmentally appropriate progress didn't involve so many potato chips.

Instead of nagging, cajoling, and lecturing, though, maybe I should try sitting back and listening for a while. That way, even without a multibillion-dollar budget and a team of shady child psychologists on my side, I'll come to understand the children's deepest hopes and fears. Marketers have seemingly endless financial resources at their disposal to get innocent little girls to buy their nasty Pop-Tarts, but they will never have access to kids' hearts and minds the way we parents do. If we see our kids as independent thinkers and hear them out with respect, maybe the bright blue packaging will lose some of its allure.

An hour after this revelation, Zack asks if he can take chips to school. "But you already have corn chips in your lunch," I point out calmly, then sit back and wait for him to continue. The listening has commenced. He reasonably explains that his friends always give him some of their snack since he usually only has something dumb in his bag, like an apple, and you can't share an apple. He needs chips — enough to distribute among a group and not look stingy.

"Can I open the potato chips?" he asks, since he's just finished off the bag of corn chips. Of course this is when I'd like to point

The Good in the Bad

Not all junk food is created equal. These alternative snack options might seem obvious, but sometimes we could all use a little reminder:

- Whole grain pretzels
- Multigrain tortilla chips (with 6 grams of fat per serving or less)
- Homemade (not microwave) popcorn. Make it in a pot with a little peanut or olive or canola oil, covered on medium-high heat. Zack likes to fancy this up with all sorts of spices. I say, Go crazy, kid.
- Low-fat frozen yogurt instead of ice cream and ice cream instead of cake or cookies or brownies. Stick to vanilla or chocolate ice cream, though—according to the rule that the fewer the ingredients on a processed food label, the better.
- Mixed nuts. Cook them with maple syrup to enhance their appeal.

out that in fact he *can* share an apple; we'd just cut it up and rub the slices with some citrus so they don't turn brown. Knowing that wouldn't go over well, though, instead I say yes.

(And yes, we still have potato chips in the house even after I've said we were going to stop stocking such stuff, mostly because I love them. Then again, I'll buy chips and leave them in the closet unopened for months — I just like having them available should I ever want them. Apparently, though, everyone else thinks that if there are snack foods in the house, it's okay to open and eat them. I find this so annoying. From now on: really, no more potato chips. I'm serious this time.)

Anyway, I say yes mostly because I find it touching that Zack wants to share with his friends, and I wonder how many similarly poignant moments I've missed out on owing to my intense focus on fighting the satanic snack companies. Besides, I have to admit that my one-woman tirade against the Snack Man has its drawbacks; even I felt just the tiniest bit embarrassed one day last year when Zack had some friends over and the kids couldn't find anything they wanted — the graham crackers were "natural," the crackers had seeds on top, and even the popcorn was blue, although fortunately, once popped and salted, it could pass. That was one time I would have been happy to have potato chips in the house. I'd forgotten just how brutal preteen boys can be.

The next morning, riding high on his chip victory from the day before, Zack badgers Andy about some jelly beans he sees in the cabinet. (Andy and I needed them for a photo shoot. My job isn't helping the cause *at all.*) Zack uses the "sharing with friends" angle again, but he doesn't have as much traction with us on that approach as he did the day before. Plus, this is candy we're talking about. As soon as the kids are at school, the leftovers go right in the trash.

That afternoon, Zack goes over to his friend Andrew's house. His mom, Holly, calls to tell me that, among other things, they made a cake, which she figured was okay because when Andrew had been at our house, we'd made french fries. I'm thinking no, we made potato chips, and there was a reason for that, but what can I say? Zack quietly tells me that he and Andrew agreed to bring something to distribute the next day, "so can I please take in some of the cake?" I knew that fryer would come back to bite me. I feel obligated to say yes.

While this isn't going as smoothly as I would have hoped — these young people are *relentless* — at least I hope that by listening I will learn more about my children. But then the next day, Saturday, Maya starts crying because I just threw out her half-eaten pizza when I was cleaning up. It's rare for us to serve something so unhealthy for lunch, or dinner for that matter, but Andy and I have been frantically decluttering the house all morning, so we didn't have time to conjure up some wholesome midday repast. Anyway, sometimes pizza happens, and at least it makes the kids happy, although Maya doesn't sound too happy right now.

"Didn't you hear me ask you to save it?" she wails, and the truth is, no, I didn't. Just like that, my self-congratulatory bubble bursts. I was too distracted thinking about what a wonderful, attentive parent I am — that, or else I was strategizing about cleaning up, preparing dinner for the friends coming over that night, getting Zack and his friend fed and watered before their indoor soccer game, making sure Maya and I would be ready to go visit our neighbors as we'd planned, and wondering what to make for dessert.

I carefully, and out of her sight, pick up an untouched piece of pizza from the very top of the trash can — it was sitting on a clean paper towel, and I'm sure restaurants do worse all the time — and put it on her plate. "I have a whole new piece for you," I tell her brightly, then add sincerely, "I'm sorry I didn't hear you." Assuaged, she sits down to eat again. A few minutes later, as I'm grabbing the broom from the back hall (which I never get the chance to actually use), I hear, "Now Mom, listen to me. *Listen.*" And Maya stops talking until she sees me turn around and look straight into her wide eyes. "I'll be back for more pizza in a few minutes, okay?" As if she's talking to a baby. "So just leave it here, okay? Did you hear me *this* time?"

It's not that I ever want or intend to be a shrew; it's just that when you're trying to raise your kids to be ethical, empathetic, thoughtful, *healthy* citizens, and it feels like basically the entire world is working to turn your kids into mindless consumers instead, it gets to you after a while. But as I work harder at really paying attention to what Zack and Maya want without immediately jumping in with judgments and comments, the effects will become far-reaching and will have a positive impact on our relationships and family life. I hope.

MISSION IMPOSSIBLE

Soon after coming up with this insight, Zack and I have a mini-fight about a Zone bar. "Dad gave me one the other day," he says with a smile. "They're *good* — especially the chocolate caramel ones." I explain that while his teacher may have told her students they should bring in a high-protein snack on the day his class has mandatory state testing — a topic for another day — she didn't mean it had to be a Zone bar, I'm sure.

Once I manage to extricate myself from this discussion before it blows up into a full-fledged fight, I decide to err on the side of quiet for the rest of the afternoon. This eventually results in a major monologue from Zack during which I am given a rare and privileged peek into the workings of his life and mind. I hear about friendships gone sour, the nice kid he's getting to know, who's sitting at his cluster of desks. It's all news to me, but I say very little in response except for the occasional supportive murmur or agreeable comment, in the wake of which more classified information about his least favorite teacher comes pouring out. This strategy *works*.

The next day I'm telling Ruth all about why I'm fired up on silence as we wait for our girls to finish gymnastics when Maya comes racing out of class breathless with excitement. "Mom," she says urgently, climbing onto my lap and looking intensely into my eyes, "Mom, *can I have a Fruit Roll-Up?*"

I look at her questioningly. "Our teacher wants to give us one," she explains. "Can I have it?"

Many thoughts are racing through my mind at this moment, none of them having anything to do with listening to what Maya wants. I look at the teacher and say politely, "She can have it, but please ask me first next time." Not only is this thing bright red — it's "cherry orange wildfire" flavor — it also has tattoos on it for my little girl's tongue.

Maya, noting my obvious displeasure, tries to soothe me. "Just so you know, my friends always have these," she says, happily smacking her lips.

"In their lunches, you mean?"

"Yeah."

That makes me feel so much better.

Fortunately, there has been one positive outcome to this Twenty-four-Hour Listening Project: while I may still be the same hard-ass when it comes to food, I am trying to pay closer attention to what the kids are saying about everything else.

One more thing to consider: if we want to have any shot at all of enticing our kids away from Cheez-Its and all they represent, we're probably going to have to compromise on step 4, the local produce issue. (That's hard to admit.) If Andy and I want the two of them eating fewer bad carbohydrates and faux-food products, we're going to have to buy at least some fruit grown out of state. Or are potato chips made in Cape Cod better than conventional melons grown half a world away?

And so, while there's still snow on the ground even though technically it's spring, I go on a mad fruit-shopping spree. I exit the store in a postfrenzy haze with nectarines, peaches, strawberries, and plums, none of it organic, most of it from another continent, none of it juicy and sweet. The kids cheer, and for the next few days, the snack fights almost disappear. But this isn't a sustainable long-term plan either, because out-of-season fruit from faraway lands, even if it's conventional and tastes like nothing and is possibly riddled with toxic chemicals, is outlandishly expensive.

PEER PRESSURE

Excellent breaking news: the intensity of the lunchtime fiasco seems to have subsided. Andy has been packing Maya *slightly* less healthy lunches than I'd like, but still ones we can all tolerate. He gives her "natural" cheese crackers along with cucumber and carrots, or dried raspberries instead of fresh apple slices. (By this time of year, the kids are getting mighty sick of apples.) "I just want her to eat," he says. Maya is thrilled.

She's also thrilled one night when Andy takes her out for Japanese food and she eats only one of her salmon roe sushi. She tells him she knows she's not supposed to have too many at one time (well, that's not it exactly), so she wants to save one for the next day's lunch. Meanwhile, George from the Monterey Bay Aquarium says he's sure it's from wild salmon, in which case it's both sustainable and clean, although it is still raw.

"You'll probably get teased by your friends," Andy warns.

"I want to freak them out," she replies.

Meanwhile, Zack has been packing his own lunches lately. It's about time. One morning when he's done, he comes over to me and tells me that, by the way, the kids have stopped teasing him. "That's great!" I exclaim. Instead of giving him lip, Zack goes on happily, the other kids can't wait to find out what he's brought. Apparently Zack's colorful salads and "natural" meat sticks have been dubbed okay.

After he's left for school, I pull the meat sticks from the fridge and read the label: "Pork and Beef Used in this Product is Wholesome, Grain Fed, & Contains NO ARTIFICIAL INGREDIENTS!"

School Lunches

- Look for lead-free lunch boxes. Reusablebags.com is where I get my kids' stuff.
- Whenever possible, pack lunches the night before and store in fridge. (I'm usually too tired to do this, but it remains a goal.)
- Offer the same food prepared in different ways, for example, carrot sticks one day and coins the next.
- Get your kids to help make their lunch or to make it themselves if they're old enough.
- Buy fancy toothpicks; these have all sorts of uses: holding a sandwich together, picking up cubed fruit, just looking fun . . .
- Put a little love note in the lunch box, or draw a heart on the napkin. (I always forget to do this.)
- Include lots of little tidbits: small containers of dried fruits and nuts, fresh berries, cheese, and crackers— make it look as varied and snacklike as possible.
- Color it up: make lunches as colorful as possible with fruits and veggies. Have theme days: orange day with carrots, pepper, orange slices, and squash soup; green day (good for the preteen set with its reference to the rock band) with cucumbers, green pepper, pickles, and kiwi; yellow day with pineapple, summer squash slices, and cheese.

I'm thinking we should put the kibosh on meat sticks when, after school, Zack says excitedly, "Mom, those meat sticks are really earning me big points!"

Me: "Oh yeah? Tell me more." At least he's not being teased anymore.

"Today I traded some for an Oreo and a piece of a granola bar." Pause. "Next I'm gonna see if I can just trade 'em for cold, hard cash."

PUT 'EM UP

What can parents do to fight back against the ubiquitous Snack Machine? As the WHO report puts it, "Bold, innovative action at both national and global levels is essential." Or, as Susan said during our talk, "Parents need to get involved with advocacy groups because this has to be changed. I know that's not what you're asking, but . . ."

Well yes, it was exactly what I was asking. It just wasn't what I wanted to hear. Come to think of it, maybe we should take this lying down after all, because fighting back sounds like it's going to take a lot of exhausting work. Still, though we might not be ready to make this our life's mission, Andy and I have at least a few tricks up our sleeve that we can use to combat the marketing fiends. Help is on the way for step 7.

First, of course, is to keep fewer snacks in the house. While we intended to try this out after talking with our pediatrician Rick nearly six years ago, potato and corn chips "somehow" kept sneaking back into the house. But now we're resolute about banning unhealthy choices and replacing them with fewer, but better, options: baked corn chips, multigrain chips. And — minor coup — we're not buying meat sticks as often, but instead of turning it into another teachable moment we're just keeping quiet. Best of all, Zack's not even grumbling about it. At least not yet. So whenever possible, eliminating onsite temptation is by far the most effective tactic of all, and it works for both kids.

As does technique number two: serve what we want them to eat, even if they haven't asked for it. For example, when Maya asks

for natural cheese crackers, I put some in a bowl along with pump- .
kin seeds, three kinds of nuts, and a few dried cranberries.

"I don't want the nuts," she complains.

"Just take a bite — you love nuts!"

"I did."

"Okay, you don't have to eat them." But when I go in to col-
lect her bowl a little while later, I see that while she has indeed
left behind the cashews and peanuts, she's eaten the almonds and
seeds (along with the crackers, obviously). Limited success. We'll
take it.

Trick number three: In a loud whisper, I "confide" that there's
only a few left of whatever I want Maya to eat, and though sometimes she'll ask why I'm whispering, this almost always works. So
just now it was plums — "This is the last one!" I said in a conspira-
torial tone. She ate it right up. We can only use this approach with
Maya, though; Zack, as a seasoned connoisseur of infomercials, is
too savvy for this approach.

And finally, Zack himself comes up with the last snack strategy,
one we're not so happy about because it means more forethought
and planning for us: he says he'll eat whatever's in the middle of
the fridge, whether it's a package of crepes or a bowl of cut-up
veggies. And since he really will, we guess we'll have to follow
through on this one. It might take a little effort, but, we admit
with a tired sigh when we see him chowing down on a bowl of
carrots, cucumbers, and peppers, it's worth it.

Chapter 7

. . . .

The Aisle Not Taken

I'm bored," I say one morning. Andy and I look at each other across the seemingly vast expanse of living room separating us. The moment drags on until Maya's happy chatter fills the space. We're planning out the week's menu, at least ostensibly, and all the usual suspects are being mentioned: pantry tacos, pasta, baked chicken . . .

Andy and I have been together for eighteen years, married for fifteen. We met as roommates in a cheap four-bedroom walk-up in Boston. When I moved in, Andy had been in the apartment for seven years, and every person who'd lived there had left at least one piece of furniture or postcollege tchotchke behind. So the front hall was watched over by a mannequin wearing three hats and two feather boas, there were four couches crammed into the small living room, and every drawer in the place was literally overflowing with stuff. The apartment may not have been a penthouse suite, but it was home.

I worked at the takeout part of Harvest, an upscale restaurant in Harvard Square. I made sandwiches and manned the cash register, but my boss also taught his team how to cook. Under his careful tutelage I learned how to whip up a mean lobster bisque, chicken roulade, and vegetable terrine. All this gourmet cooking definitely piqued my interest in food, but after work I subsisted on affordable but dreary frozen ravioli and plain yogurt. Soon enough, though, when I came home from work, my roommate Andy began surprising me with meals of succulent grilled swordfish (before we knew of its multiple evils) and aromatic Cincinnati beef chili (ditto). (And yes, he'll eat Cincinnati chili, even though it's stewlike and has tomato paste in it. What can I say, the man's an enigma.) This was the same guy who kept his rusty old Datsun running by using tomato paste cans as a tailpipe; in other words, he may not have seemed like the fine-dining type, but he was a fantastic cook and he wooed me with food.

We spent blissful hours wandering various neighborhoods — Boston's Italian North End, Chinatown — always in search of ingredients. We would come home with lobster and cookies, pork ribs and rice noodles, then turn them into a home-cooked banquet. This is all to say that, in the beginning, our life together was easy and peaceful. We were well rested and supremely well fed.

Of course, that was then. This is now.

THE MORE THINGS CHANGE . . .

When the four of us started this makeover last fall, Andy and I had already weathered our share of marital storms, so we were confident we'd emerge from this stronger than ever. After all, as someone who not only appreciates food but also was a onetime nuclear power plant protester, Andy would seem to be just the kind of guy to care about toxins in our food supply. But it's become abundantly clear in the past few months that his dietary peccadilloes are far more powerful than his interest in a better diet.

Andy's folks were visiting recently, when the subject of their son's eating habits came up. We were discussing his former vegetarianism (a droll diet for a guy who doesn't eat many vegetables), along with the fact that he didn't used to like onions. That one was news to me. Even this late in the game, married life is full of surprises. They then told me that Andy's food preferences have changed a lot since he met me. Now, his dad said, "He eats anything and everything."

In a way I could see what they were saying. The schoolboy they once knew had the same lunch every day for years: peanut butter crackers, Fritos, and carrot sticks. And now this stranger in front of them eats swordfish, steak, even onions? Although, come to think of it, they might not know that most of this had nothing to do with me. For example, once Andy moved to Boston for college and was no longer landlocked, he became a seafood fiend. That was long before I came on the scene. But it is true that his adventurous spirit kicked up a notch during our honeymoon in France, where he tried the likes of pâté and tapenade, and where we both fell madly in love with cheese. Before France, it had mostly been American or bust for Andy.

That reminds me of the night we found ourselves in a magical Provençal garden enjoying yet another simple but flawless French dinner. Feeling heady and adventurous and maybe a bit tipsy on local wine, we decided to end our meal with a cheese course, and since neither of us knew anything about the subject, we grandly told our server in halting French that we'd take whatever he recommended.

The small lump he ceremoniously placed in front of us a few minutes later turned out to be the most pungent supposedly edible item we'd ever paid for. The odor immediately wafted up from the plate, drowning out the garden's intoxicating twin aromas of lavender and rosemary; I smiled feebly at our waiter until, satisfied, he turned and walked away. We never figured out whether he was just going for a good laugh at the expense of the dopey Americans, but inspired by the ancient Roman sites we'd seen that day in Arles, Andy dubbed this cheese the Toe of Augustus, which, we posited, might have been freshly unearthed just hours ago from a nearby gravesite. We quickly devolved into guffawing American boors.

In other words, once he was a married man, Andy went straight from Kraft singles right to the Toe of Augustus, and even though he didn't so much as touch the latter with his fork, it was still a drastic shift. I can see where this transformation might bewilder his parents and leave them thinking I'm the one to credit — or blame. But non-American cheese, all types of olives and onions notwithstanding, I must lovingly disagree with Andy's parents on two points: first, I believe Andy's culinary horizons would have expanded with or without me, and, second, I insist that their son is still basically impossible when it comes to food.

Of course, I don't want to come off as the obnoxious daughter-in-law — Andy's folks already think I'm a little nutty; after all, they've seen us grocery shopping, which is like having them see us in our underwear. So when they talk about how many foods he likes these days, I heroically keep my mouth shut and nod politely. But now that my in-laws are safely back in Ohio, I feel free to reiterate that Andy won't eat:

> All condiments (including ketchup, mustard, and mayo)
> Casseroles of any kind
> Cheese, soft: cream, blue, ricotta, fresh mozzarella (He
>   only used to eat American, but now he's branched out;
>   these four are still verboten, though.)
> Cilantro
> Dessert (except very occasionally)
> Lots of seafood (clams, mussels, oysters, bluefish, etc.)

Many vegetables, too numerous to list

Most sauces (including barbeque, gravy, mustard, and
   cream)

Most stews (unless he's made them, and even then he'll
   carefully pick out the meat and leave the wet parts
   behind)

Oatmeal

Pickles (unless he's made them)

Sour cream

Squash (winter, summer)

Tofu

Tomatoes in any form (fresh, dried, sauce, etc.)

Vinegar

Yogurt

It's not just that he doesn't like these foods; it's that if someone
were to force him to have one of them, it would traumatize him.
Once in a while he'll make an effort by taking a tiny bite out of
a tomato or a nibble of squash, but his flared nostrils and long-
suffering silence afterward tell me all I need to know. I try to be
understanding, but it's hard. I'm married to a man who won't eat
tomatoes.

And so, when Andy and I are sitting in the living room talking about the week's menu and he keeps mentioning the same old
options, I get mad. I am also feeling a little worried about Maya.
In *The Omnivore's Dilemma*, Michael Pollan writes that there
"seems to be an evolutionary trade-off between big brains and big
guts — two very different evolutionary strategies for dealing with
the question of food selection. The case of the koala bear, one of
nature's pickiest eaters, exemplifies the small-brain strategy. You
don't need a lot of brain circuitry to figure out what's for dinner

when all you ever eat is eucalyptus leaves." I really want Maya to try a new food this week.

MENU PLANNING: FROM ANGER TO ACCEPTANCE

Just as all this dust is being kicked up, a funny thing happens. I open an e-mail: "Be part of an exciting press trip to experience the unique cuisine and attractions of Macau." The offer is tempting: a press trip to Macau, where I'd stay in expensive hotels, eat gourmet food that will almost certainly include vinegar and tomatoes, and get treated like a VIP, all for free.

On the other hand, a press trip to Macau where I'd spend the days with public relations types, then whore myself out when it comes time to write it up.

Let's see. Macau versus ethics, ethics versus Macau . . . It's a tough one, to be sure. That night as I'm still mulling over the invitation, Zack is in the bathroom brushing his teeth. Maya wants in, and Zack is holding the door closed.

Maya: "Zackie, if you don't let me in, I'll pee on your butt." Andy makes him open the door. Next, Zack says something that is unintelligible to us but clearly unkind, to which Maya replies, "If you don't stop, I'll spit in your eyeball."

Zack taunts, "C'mon, here's an open target," at which point Maya actually spits on the floor, then asks, "Did I get any in your eyeball or on the tip of your nose?" This particular fight doesn't end in tears, shouts, or slammed doors, but too many other times they do.

Still, for every one of these little spats, there's a hug, a kiss, a belly laugh that I can't stand to miss if I don't have to, and the years are just racing by . . . Plus, what would I do for ten days

Grocery Shopping Strategies

- Whenever possible, leave the kids at home.
- Agree on what you will and won't buy before you leave the house.
- In stores that have a seating area, go at mealtime and set the kids up with something healthy from the prepared-foods counter (if they're old enough, you can go off without them; if not, one parent shops while the other one stays with the kids).
- In my house, when Maya asked for a box of sugar cereal, I told her she could have it for dessert. By now she's been so programmed that she amiably replied, "Of course."
- Let each kid choose something from the produce aisle. This is a good way to get kids involved and maybe, just maybe, if they pick it out, they'll actually try it.

without Maya's kisses on the nose? Or one of Zack's formidable veggie omelets with tomatoes, mushrooms, and chives that he serves me in bed? Not that often, it's true, but if I were away, I'm sure I wouldn't just want a Zack omelet and a kiss from Maya, I'd need them.

I decide that sadly, for now it's Macau: 0. Hugs, fights, and breakfast in bed: 3. When Zack hears I've turned down the trip, he quietly and sincerely tells me how glad he is; later, on a day that's not as sunny for the two of us, he will wonder if anyone's invited me on a trip a little farther *away* than Far East Asia is.

So instead of an exciting, all-expenses paid trip to parts unknown, we're off to Whole Foods for another morning of shopping. As we're standing in front of the fresh pasta, I ask Maya, "How about the brown ones?"

"You're just saying that because they're healthier," she says accusingly. "I'm getting these," and she picks up a package of plain white pasta and stomps off to the cart. Next, I inspect a package of sweet potato gnocchi until Maya says she won't eat them, and Andy and Zack say *maybe* they'll try them, at which point I breathe out loudly in the manner of a martyr and put them back.

All the usual suspects get piled into the cart — broccoli, apples, white pasta, with the nutritionist's advice about eating a *variety* of fruits and vegetables still ringing in my ears, when I see Andy coming to the cart with — what's this — a chayote? I must have really scared him earlier with my comments about being bored, because he hates all squash equally, no matter what continent it hails from.

"Why'd you get that?" I ask in a somewhat unfriendly tone.

"Just trying something new," he says, exasperated. But we both know his heart isn't in it, so it's just not the same.

I could take matters into my own hands and cook up a banquet of delights all for myself, but the goal here is to serve family dinners that work for everyone, and while I know the answer won't be found in the likes of chayote, I haven't given up on this elusive goal yet.

So one day, when we're planning the menu for a Sunday lunch with friends, I go through cookbook upon cookbook until I come across a recipe for an Italian soup made with chickpeas and pork short ribs that I think everyone will like. I'll be happy because it uses meat as a condiment and because it's something different,

Andy will be happy because there will be no tomatoes or vinegar, Zack will like the short ribs, and Maya will eat the chickpeas. "Whaddya think?" I ask Andy excitedly.

He's silent at first, then he gives a notably muted, "That sounds fine."

"What's wrong with it?" I ask in growing irritation. The two of us have been here thousands of times before: I get my culinary hopes up, only to have them dashed by my persnickety husband.

"Nothing. I'm just not sure if our friends keep kosher." Why would he think this couple keeps kosher? Just because they're Jewish? He knows better than that. Besides, the husband is a chef, and I can't imagine a kosher chef working in a nonkosher restaurant.

But now that he's brought up the possibility, how can I argue? I've proposed serving a potentially unsacred meal to our friends, which would not only be offensive but also an embarrassment to us all. We could call and ask if they do in fact keep kosher but clearly for some unknown reason Andy doesn't want to make the Italian soup, so I back off. Instead, he presents me with a recipe for white bean and garlic soup, to which I amiably agree. The next morning, we stop at the store for ingredients — the kids and I stay in the car — and Andy emerges with the beans and stock we need for the soup.

"What's this?" I ask, pointing to a package of some kind of meat wrapped in paper.

"Bacon."

My eyebrows go up as high as they can. *Bacon?* I ask incredulously.

"For flavor," he answers reasonably.

"Guess you're not worried about whether they keep kosher anymore," I say bitingly.

"It's just a control thing," he says with a shrug. "Admit it."

"*Me* admit it?" I ask, and by now we're both laughing. He always does this — disarms me with humor — and unfortunately, it works. I'm left laughing when in a fairer world I would be winning points to use against him. Of course, the soup he makes is delicious, it most definitely needed a little bacon to deepen its flavor, and our friends, who don't keep kosher, love it.

The next weekend, we have our friends Robin, Jeff, and their kids over for dinner. Ever hopeful, the day before I find yet another recipe that everyone will like; or they *should* anyway: Cambodian pork stir-fry with butternut squash. I figure Andy can just pick around the squash, although admittedly I'm really thinking, Why the hell won't you eat a little squash, for Christ's sake? But when I tell him the name of the dish, the same thing happens again: Andy isn't biting. He says that instead, he wants ribs and chicken wings.

Normally, I give in, as I did with the Italian soup, or else get irritable, like I'm about to right now, but no matter what I'll always drop the matter quickly, because if we're looking at the big picture of our marriage, I know I have it damn good. But this time I do neither of the above; instead I gently point out that, once again, he's directed the discussion and the menu away from what I love and toward what he loves. He looks dismayed.

"I didn't mean to do that," he says. "I'm sorry." And yet he doesn't give in. He insists that for this meal with Robin and her family, we make the pork with squash, and the ribs, and the wings. At the very least still wanting to preserve the Asian bent to the meal, I add ginger and five-spice powder to the dry rub for the ribs. We then agree to glaze the wings with a sweet teriyaki marinade. Just to round things out, we also serve green beans with chili paste and organic basmati rice.

Robin and Jeff rave about every single bite, only lending credence to Andy's unwieldy, meat-centric approach, and I'm left thinking that despite the apology, by insisting on making all three dishes he is being more than a tiny bit willful. Then again, maybe this is his way of asserting himself in the midst of what's undeniably turned into a mealtime maelstrom. I'm also left with a question: isn't food made with love supposed to taste better? Because this three-meat dinner was prepared with more than a soupçon of resentment — at least on my part — and it's still delectable.

Upon further reflection, while I may wish Andy would change, he's not going to, and when push comes to shove, I don't need him to. I guess in the end I'm probably the one who has to change by accepting my husband as he is. This must be what the rabbi meant by "for better or worse" all those years ago. I should have paid more attention to what he was saying.

A few days later, at the end of a long, aimless, out-of-sorts day, I go over to Andy, sitting on the couch, peacefully leafing through an alternative energy magazine, and I straddle him, pushing my forehead into his. We hold our hands up, palms together.

"Let's get crazy," he says, and I look at him expectantly. He drops his voice — after all, there are kids crawling all over the house — and when I lean in closer, he whispers, "Let's trade pants." What can I say? Even if his eating habits drive me insane, I love this man.

JUST THE TWO OF US

What we need is a nice, long vacation in the sun, just the two of us, away from all the quarrels and menu planning and cold weather. But that's not realistic, so instead I change the fantasy to the four of us, which quickly morphs into the six of us, because we'd also want to take Stacia and her boyfriend so Andy and I could slip away for a couple hours now and then. St. Bart's would be nice, although we've always wanted to see the U.S. Virgin Islands . . .

Of course, there's no trip at all in our near future; we've already told the kids that the last week of the summer is going to be a "vacation from home!" That's because last year we stayed in a rental house in Westport, Massachusetts, that reeked of mold and mildew; it was a "holiday" that generally made us all miserable in different ways: the kids were grumpy because the TV broke, Zack didn't have his own room, I couldn't breathe owing to the stench, etcetera ad nauseam. We also have Roxy to consider; assuming and hoping she's still with us, we wouldn't feel right about shipping her off to a kennel or inflicting her on Stacia. Fortunately, our false enthusiasm has worked its magic, because Zack has mentioned a couple of times how excited he is for our vacation-from-home.

But it becomes evident that our tactics haven't had quite the self-hypnotic effect we would wish for when one morning I find Andy poring over a *National Geographic Expeditions* catalog.

"Anything look good?" I ask.

"There are some great trips in here," he says. "There's a photographic expedition in Tuscany I'd like to take." He looks down at the magazine for a minute, flips through a bunch of pages, then stops and looks up at me. "I know you won't go sailing," he says, "but how about a barge trip in France? That shouldn't be too bad."

"Sure," I agree with an animated nod. "I'd love to go on a barge trip in France." Then I squint my eyes and get up close to his face. "What are you *talking* about?"

I know, a married father of two has to dream; take that away and what does he have left? Andy and I are constantly sublimating our own desires to accommodate the realities of parenthood, so while we may yearn for a week on Fantasy Island or in Tuscany or Provence, we'll settle for an hour in a Motel 6. In reality, though, we know we're not going anywhere other than the grocery store or maybe, if we're lucky, out to dinner.

Then it hits me: maybe we need to forget about the kids for a little bit, because, frankly, they're wearing us down with their resistance. For example, Maya's in the kitchen. With her brow furrowed and mouth gaping wide, she is shouting out in agony, "I hate falafel!" Her whole little body tenses against the mere thought of it. Of course, Maya has never *tried* falafel.

"Taste this," I command, pulling a crispy piece off of one of the balls cooling on the paper towel. She takes a tiny bite. No reaction.

"I think I'll take another taste," she says delicately.

"Do you like it?" I ask.

"It's all right," she concedes, then makes a so-so motion with her hands.

"But will you *eat* it?" I push.

"Maybe."

This kind of scene day after day, even hour after hour, slowly but surely erodes our upbeat spirits. Over time, it even sets Andy and me at odds with each other because when it's dinnertime and everyone's hungry and we're not sure what we'll do if Maya won't eat the falafel, we get cranky, and then we start in on each other.

So when Maya leaves the room while we finish making dinner, I anxiously whisper to Andy, "What if she won't eat it?"

"I don't know," he says irritably. He's busy cooking in hot oil at the moment. "Cereal?" he asks distractedly.

"But that's not healthy!" I answer with a worried frown.

"I don't know, babe," he then says tersely, and I walk away to set the table.

Andy and I need it to be us against the world again. That's how it used to be in our rose-colored past, and I'm pretty sure it's how it can be once more, only now it also needs to be us against the *kids,* because it's become obvious I can't win them over until the two of us are on the same team again.

Amazingly, within an hour of this revelation, a book comes in the mail. Not just any book, but one called *InterCourses,* featuring recipes for known aphrodisiacs. We take it as a sign and book ourselves a night at a hotel in Cambridge. It's just what the doctor ordered.

SOON AFTER WE get back, Maya comes down with a fever, thereby providing yet more proof of my theory that anytime we parents have a good time without our children, we pay for it with an illness of some sort. The ratio turns out to be about six days of fever (or throwing up) per day of parental freedom. One day during Maya's predictably weeklong flu, Andy brings home Strawberry Shortcake videos for her.

He has something for me too: a video called *The Future of Food,* which looks into the "disturbing truth behind the unlabeled, patented, genetically engineered foods that have quietly filled grocery store shelves for the past decade." The film "gives a voice to farmers whose lives and livelihoods have been negatively impacted by this new technology." It examines "the complex web of market and political forces that are changing what we eat as huge multinational corporations seek to control the world's food system."

I look up at him through glassy eyes from the couch and laugh weakly. I myself am not feeling so well. I'm not sick as Maya is, but I'm aching, probably from angst over what we've been learning since we started working on this family meal makeover. Whose idea was this again?

"Think I'll take a pass on this one," I mumble.

"Are you serious?" he asks. "I thought this would be great for you! Who knows what you'll learn."

"Thanks, I don't think so."

In fact, I don't want to think about any of it — fiber, fatty acids, feedlots, fossil fuels, or environmental degradation — for even *one more second*. I need a break.

A SIDE OF CAR

"I've been thinking," Andy begins one evening, and that makes *me* think: Uh-oh. When Andy turned forty, he'd been thinking about drum lessons, and soon enough we had two used drum sets and a carpenter coming over to soundproof a small room in the basement. Another time he had been thinking we ended up with Zack; five years later, Andy's muse led us to Maya. And this time? It seems that he has been *thinking* about fossil fuels, solar panels, and electric cars. "Even Zack said he's learning that fossil fuels are going to run out in this century," Andy tells me. "The technology exists for us to be virtually self-sufficient."

My practical businessman husband wants off the grid?

This is on a Friday evening. By Sunday morning, less than forty-eight hours later, he says he's found a used car for sale. I knew we were interested in a used car, but I didn't know we were interested in one *right now*. We've been talking about hybrids for a while, although neither of us is really impressed with them. Still, if it were up to me, we almost certainly would have ended up with one. It turns out it wasn't.

The car he's found is a twenty-two-year-old Mercedes that runs on vegetable oil; the owner needs to sell it immediately because he's moving to DC in three days, so he's willing to bargain.

Restaurants are usually happy to give their used oil away because then they don't have to pay for its removal. Plus, the emissions smell like fries. What's not to love?

And so by Tuesday afternoon we're the proud owners of one old, sweet dark blue Benz, all because Andy got a bee in his bonnet. This is the same man who keeps telling me he's a baby steps kind of guy? Apparently that designation only applies to food; when it comes to frybrids, he's a maniac.

Meanwhile, he's also looking into solar panels; has ordered a solar iPod charger — he's even found cheap land in Nova Scotia. "We could put a yurt up there," he says. "Then we'd officially be fringy freaks." Clearly, work has been slow lately. Andy wants to be like one of those rich celebrities with too much time on his hands so he could pursue all of his projects without any financial worries. He also wants a "cabana boy" to filter and change the vegetable oil for him, and we haven't even owned the car for a day. I smell trouble.

The reason this car makes sense, at least to Andy and the kids, is that because it runs on used oil they can justify bringing the fryer back up from the basement. The other reason it makes sense is that Andy's car is very old and has about 150,000 miles on it.

The reason it doesn't, though? The Mercedes, at 210,000 miles, has far more. And there's another potential problem: by driving our car, we might be committing a felony, if Massachusetts is anything like Illinois, where a retired frybrid-owning couple in their late seventies found two men from the Department of Revenue on their doorstep one morning, one of whom was actually a senior agent in the Bureau of Criminal Investigations. The couple's so-called crime? Not paying motor fuel tax. I tell Andy that before anyone finds out about our car, he'd best check out the law in

Massachusetts; I'd hate to go to prison or pay a stiff fine because we're trying to clean up the earth.

I'm starting to understand what it must be like when your partner gets all jazzed up about something, and while you think it's basically dope and fly and all that, you also can't help wondering *what's gotten into him*. I suppose in a way we're each having our own version of a midlife crisis, but at least we're trying to channel all that intense energy in ways that will enhance, and not hurt, our relationship. For example, Andy's grease car will keep him off the streets and in the basement filtering oil where he belongs, and while I'm not so sure he is equally glad about my food-based approach since it impinges more on family harmony and mealtimes, that's life. And marriage.

Meanwhile, Zack is looking at his ol' dad with renewed respect and interest. I make sure to drive it home that the car and solar panels and yurts are Daddy's way of trying to make the world a better place, and that mine is by focusing on what we eat.

"What can I do to help?" Zack asks.

"Empty the dishwasher?" I offer.

"Turn out the lights in your room," Andy says more sincerely.

Zack rolls his eyes at both suggestions.

"We're serious," I say, launching into a lecture about the importance of turning off lights we're not using, though I let the dishwasher thing slide.

A few days after we've bought our Benz, we finish up a Whole Foods excursion shaking our heads in distress after having been walloped with a particularly exorbitant bill. Andy then says reassuringly, "Don't worry, our food bills are about to go down because we're going to have a greenhouse. I've been looking into that too."

"Awesome!" I say, playing along. "We need it."

"Mom," Zack says, laughing, "you thought Dad was serious?" We have about .01 acre of arable land surrounding our house.

"I am," interjects Andy. "Soon enough, we'll be living in a geodesic biosphere."

The conversation has officially turned silly. Later that night, when Andy and I have put the kids to bed and we're talking about the car, he admits he's a little apprehensive — picking up and filtering the oil is no small job, he solemnly informs me. But then, he adds more cheerfully, "It's just like doing the laundry." Andy hasn't done the laundry since before I met him. And as one who actually does, I can say that to me, double-filtering vegetable oil for a car sounds far worse. So we'll see.

Of course I'd be happier if Andy woke up one day and suddenly loved all foods and whole grains; then we would climb into our grease car and drive off into the sunset talking about the eggplant with peanuts and quinoa pilaf we'd make for dinner. But none of that's happening — except, oddly, for the grease car part.

No matter, because suddenly I look at my husband of a decade and a half and realize that in fact we can always find a middle ground, with the operative word being *middle*. He may still hanker after swordfish and sirloin, but at least now he's willing to reconsider both of those. And I may not be willing to filter dirty oil in the basement, but that too could change someday. Ultimately, though, as long as we keep working together, everything's going to be just fine — unless, that is, one of us gets another crazy idea.

Chapter 8

Do It Yourself (or Not)

DIRTY, DISEASE-RIDDEN, AND DELICIOUS

We're now ready for step 8 of our makeover: poultry. At least, I'm ready; Andy might be surprised to learn that lately I've been thinking we should raise chickens.

That's because while we're doing pretty well finding local beef, pork, and eggs, it's still hard to source poultry that's truly free range, humanely raised, and clean. Chicken is one of our family's main sources of protein, and according to the USDA, we're not alone; per capita chicken consumption in the United States has increased forty pounds in the past three and a half decades to about sixty pounds a year. When I mention the possibility of keeping birds in the yard, Andy's not amused. He shakes his head. It's a nonnegotiable no. And I'm actually scared to talk about it with Zack and Maya; if they heard me so much as mention it, they'd likely vote me out of the house. What's she gonna do next? they might think. Compost sewage?

But then one morning when Maya and I are at Ruth's house, I learn I'm not the only one who has chicken coops on her mind. Ruth's eleven-year-old daughter, Susanna, has just come back from a two-night field trip to the Farm School. "Did you meet Roy?" I ask her excitedly, and she nods enthusiastically but wordlessly — I think she has something sweet in her mouth that she's trying to hide from her parents. Once she's swallowed the evidence, the two of us rave about Roy for a couple minutes; then she tells me that she talked with him about her lifelong desire to keep chickens.

Who knew that the daughter of one of my very best friends and I share this (peculiar) desire in common? My own kids might not appreciate the beauty of chickens, but at least Susanna does. They even seem kind of manageable; how much harder can they be than, say, an old, sick dog and two nonstop eaters? Besides, they're nothing like the four betta fish and three hermit crabs we've killed over the years, I'm sure of it.

As Susanna and I wax poetic about live fowl, Ruth's husband, Andrew, wanders over and starts listening in. "I've even talked about it with Andy!" I tell them, and then I relate the conversation, which went something like:

Me, longingly: "I wish we could raise chickens."

Andy, huffily: "You mean, you want *me* to raise chickens."

Me: "Well, obviously I want *you* to raise chickens." Then, for some reason, I tell Andrew and Susanna with a shrug, Andy just shook his head and walked away. Andrew fixes his big blue eyes right on me and says, "Andy is a *very nice man.*" Then he bursts out laughing. I'm thinking, What's so funny?

A lengthy, animated discussion ensues, in which Susanna and I go on dreamily about how great it would be to have our own chickens — for eggs only, of course, since neither of us is much into killing live animals, "although . . ." I say, gazing into the distance as I envision confidently yet compassionately slashing the neck of what could become a rich coq au vin or possibly the best fried chicken ever. Then I imagine the blood on my hands, and bits of plucked feathers sticking to the bottoms of my shoes, and Zack asking for a divorce from me. Susanna breaks what has be-

Good Food Books for Kids

Baby–Preschool
Lunch, by Denise Fleming

Ages 3–5
Eating the Alphabet: Fruits & Vegetables from A to Z, by
Lois Ehlert

Ages 3–6
Apples and Pumpkins, by Anne Rockwell

Ages 4–8
A Fruit and Vegetable Man, by Roni Schotter
Growing Vegetable Soup, by Lois Ehlert
Veggie Soup, by Dorothy Donohue

Ages 10–14
Made You Look, by Shari Graydon. In fun, down-to-earth
writing, it offers a kid-friendly look into advertising. It's
also a great way to start an ongoing discussion.

Here are some fun Web site games and activities for kids
that promote healthy foods: www.bam.gov
www.cdc.gov/powerfulbones
www.mypyramid.gov/kids

come sort of a nightmarish spell by informing me we could legally
keep the birds inside the house, and while doing so would definitely make things easier with the neighbors, this is where even I
have to draw the line.

When Maya and I get home from Ruth and Andrew's house, I
tell Andy the good news: We can probably raise chickens here!

"I don't think so," he says, shaking his head. "It's illegal."

"But Ruth thinks we can."

"Let her do it then."

"No, no, Ruth and Andrew don't want to do it, Susanna does. It's just that they think we *can*."

"I think they're wrong," he says flatly, but then he adds a little more kindly, "Let's stick to produce." I really have no right to say anything because without Andy even our houseplants would be dead. Andy's a born gentleman farmer; he's been gardening for years on our tiny plot of land right by the street. Last year he planted asparagus and he's excited to see if they happen this year — *happen* is the correct horticultural term, right? — but he says it's too early to call on the grapes.

"You planted grapes?" I ask. He laughs, presumably at my ignorance.

"Last season. And don't forget about the mushrooms." I had indeed forgotten about the logs he inoculated with shiitake, which he's hoping will sprout this year. Despite all his efforts, though, until we move to a farm in the country, which will never happen, we'll have to make do with other people's crops since ours aren't going to yield enough to feed anything larger than a squirrel, although we do keep those in fat city.

The next time Susanna comes over to our house, she proudly hands me a printout with specifications for legally keeping fowl, which she researched by herself on the Internet. This girl is clearly ready for the heady responsibility of poultry ownership. By reading the document carefully and eyeballing the distance to our neighbors' houses, it seems that there is one spot on our lot where we could legally keep up to four chickens.

"I think two would be good," I hedge, wondering if I might have gone too far with this whole thing. I mean, what if we really *are* allowed to keep chickens? "Susanna, where'd you get this info?" I ask her. We go into my office and she finds the Web site; we quickly realize that these regulations apply to a town in Texas.

"Darn!" (Phew!)

Still, it seems like it might be possible. We won't get the final answer until a few days later when budding investigative reporter Susanna will call to report that "unfortunately, raising chickens *isn't* allowed here" — so that night, while it's still up in the air, after the kids are in bed and things have quieted down, I lovingly, peaceably ask Andy about chickens.

"They're dirty and disease ridden," he says, and I'm nodding, thinking, Yeah, so are children. Go on. But then he lowers his voice and adds, "What about bird flu?" Now he's getting ugly but also more efficient. He knows I don't want to be cleaning up a nasty, possibly contaminated chicken coop and worrying about a deadly pandemic. And so I have to give up on getting live fowl and a cute urban coop for my birthday this week. Instead, ready to move on to a different step 8, I have another request.

ICE, ICE BABY

I'm on the phone with my friend Smitha. My birthday has gotten off to a good start, I tell her; the kids have showered me with hugs and kisses, along with breakfast in bed. "And," I go on, "the three of them got me a new freezer for the basement!"

A few hours earlier when they'd given me the coupon for the freezer, Andy told me that he and Maya bought it when I'd taken Zack and his friend Andrew to Boston's Museum of Science for the morning.

"Remember?" he asked.

Yeah, I remembered. While Andy and Maya were at Sears, the two boys and I had been immersed in the museum's hands-on animation exhibit and the amazing, but also disturbing, AI dog. When it was time for lunch, Zack and Andrew each wanted an individual pizza, soda, and fries. Naturally, I wanted to order them salad and a bottle of water, but instead I told them they could have pizza and either soda or fries. Andrew chose fries and Zack got soda; when Andrew generously offered to share, Zack ended up helping himself to the fries too. As we ate there were so many questions running through my mind: First, why do children's museums allow the likes of McDonald's and the equivalent in their food courts? Would pizza and fries be okay with Andrew's parents? Was I embarrassing Zack by setting a limit? Was I bumming Andrew out?

Anyway, I tell Smitha, amazingly, Maya kept the freezer a secret for more than a week. "Isn't that great?"

Smitha asks me what I have planned for the day.

"I'm having coffee with Ruth — but maybe you didn't hear me? They bought me a freezer for the basement."

"I heard you," she says. "I just didn't have anything to say to that."

Smitha is my best friend from college. She has the soul of a poet and film-star looks; somehow, though, she ended up becoming a radiation oncologist whose days are filled with tragic and untimely deaths. I don't know what she wants for her birthday, but it's absolutely not a major appliance. To me, though, a new freezer means that maybe we *can* have our cake and eat it too.

I only mean this metaphorically, as evidenced by the icy remnants of Zack's ice-cream cake from last year sitting forlornly in the old, decrepit fridge/freezer in the basement that we're getting rid of. This year, once we were done with Zack's birthday cake for the evening, Andy put it on the top back stair since he didn't feel like taking all those irksome steps into the basement just yet. He thought it would be fine for a few minutes — it was o degrees out — but apparently he didn't place it on the stair carefully because suddenly I heard him cry, "Oh no!" The cake had careened down the stairs, *splat.* I liked his approach to getting rid of leftover cake.

When it comes to preserving food *other than* cake, I'm sorely tempted by canning, but I had to give that up after nearly offing my beloved grandfather, Poppy, when he was a mere eighty years old. Fortunately, he had my grandmother call me before trying any of the lovingly made strawberry jam from the jar with the bulging top. "Throw it out!" I exclaimed, and he went on to live another ten years. No thanks to me.

I figure even I can handle freezing foods to preserve them, though. We've been freezing just-picked raspberries for the last few years, and when we've actually remembered to use them, it's been amazing. And when we haven't: icy raspberry clumps that give us pangs of regret.

But that's not going to happen anymore, because this freezer represents a new beginning. We are about to regain a semblance of control over what we eat. We will have ownership of our life and parenting. We will take back power from the Man. This is no less than freezer love.

It's planet love too, because this freezer has the Energy Star seal of approval. Consider this from the Energy Star Web site, a joint program run by the EPA and the U.S. Department of Energy: "If just one in 10 homes used Energy Star qualified appliances, the change would be like planting 1.7 million new acres of trees. Americans, with the help of Energy Star, saved enough energy in 2006 alone to avoid greenhouse gas emissions equivalent to those from 25 million cars — all while saving $14 billion on their utility bills."

Not only will we save money, but we can finally become true locavores! (And now I know where we'll be putting all those over-sized bags of fair-trade coffee.) We'll be able to enjoy a taste of summer during next winter's first nor'easter; as the storm rages outside, we'll be snuggled up in front of the fire, a bowlful of local eggplant, okra, and pumpkin stew in our hands.

Of course, no one but me will be eating it, and if I really did serve that dish the kids would have something else in mind — say, my head on a platter . . . So in some ways, the freezer doesn't represent a new beginning after all; in fact, maybe it's just another manifestation of one mother's quixotic dream. Still, Andy, Zack, and Maya would certainly be willing to try some local ham and corn. That would be a start.

The freezer is delivered on a sunny Tuesday morning, and within a half-hour it's ready to roll. (Symbolically anyway — because while it was supposed to come with wheels, the delivery guys forgot them. Three months, three visits from Sears, and countless phone calls later, it's still not fixed. Angry Andy: "Customer service is dead in America.")

Once the freezer is here, and before we make Sears come take it back so we can buy a different one from Home Depot where the service will be spot-on, I start reading up on freezing and quickly cross paths with disaster-preparedness types. While they certainly have their (scary) point of view, we're looking at this more from the "organic local burger for the grill" perspective rather than the "dried milk for End Times" approach. Then again, after spending a few too many minutes on that last Web site, we might just go ahead and buy a couple extra gallons of water for the basement.

I get off the apocalyptic Web sites and back into the food-

Freezing Foods

. . . .

For more information about freezing foods, see these
Web sites:

www.ext.nodak.edu/extnews/askext/freezing.htm
http://www.uga.edu/nchfp/how/freeze.html

preservation mainstream, which is when I learn that while we've
merrily been freezing food for most of our lives, we've been doing it all wrong. Who knew that store-bought meat had to be
"overwrapped," that is, wrapped again, before freezing because
the store packaging isn't "moisture-vapor resistant"? Okay, it's
true. I've read this before. It's just that until now, I've chosen to
ignore it.

Minimal research turns up reams of material: lists and charts
and graphs of how long to steam or boil vegetables and how long
you can store them once you're done. One of us might need a PhD
in microbiology in order to fully understand it all, but luckily no
one said we have to understand it, only that we need to be able
to follow directions. I bet we can handle freezing. I'm sure we
can. The kids deserve it, even if they don't much care about any
of this.

Since there's no local produce to be had just yet, for now we'll
have to focus on meats and fish. Luckily, Andy and I have found
a couple nearby farms that sell frozen meat at half the cost of
fresh, and while it won't be as delicious as Lionette's product, it
will be good enough. And easy — with meat there's no blanching
required, as there is for vegetables and fruits. We can just throw

the already-frozen, double-wrapped bundles into the freezer and walk away.

I then do some more reading about freezing fish, and once I do I decide to ignore that section, both because we're not about to eat any fish we catch (not that we even go fishing) and also because preparing seafood for the freezer supposedly requires a lemon-gelatin or ice glaze. If there's any glazing to be done in this house, it will need to involve cake.

Although I just remembered, we have two pounds of tilapia in the freezer, all in the original wrapping, all in one huge clump. Shoot. Has it been in there too long? Is it wrecked? The wrapping paper has a little red splotch on it — what from? — but assuming it's harmless, and since the package has only been in there for a couple months and we supposedly have up to four more, I decide to give it a try rather than let time roll by and then just throw it out as we usually would.

Technically, the powers-that-be say we could cook it when it's still frozen, but I'm pretty sure that wouldn't work once it's become a solid mass of fillets. So with fingers crossed and hopes low, I put the mass into the fridge; the plan is to make tilapia fish sticks based on a KidSafe recipe from chef Sara Moulton.

Thirty hours later, miracle of miracles, the fish is defrosted. I carefully pull the paper back and none sticks. I run the fillets under cold water and they come apart perfectly. Things are going swimmingly so far, and if I weren't pathologically incapable of following a recipe, I'm sure the fish would have tasted great too. Unfortunately, though, it ends up kind of bland and floppy, because instead of cutting the fillets into "fingers" so each one could get crispy on all sides, I kept them whole. Big mistake. I often omit and substitute crucial ingredients and steps with abandon when I'm "following" a recipe, and it usually turns out fine. Not always, though.

In my defense, as I was dredging fish through milk and flour and bread crumbs, Maya was on the couch with a fever, weakly calling out, "Mommy, come back here," which soon enough got shortened to, "Mommy, *come*."

The next night I remember there's some wild sockeye salmon in the freezer too. Unfortunately, after we bought it we saw that KidSafe doesn't recommend sockeye salmon because of PCBs, but Environmental Defense says it's fine, so that's who we're going with this time. We bought the salmon already frozen, so at least we know it's been packaged properly, glazed or iced or whatever. Then I remember I need to tell Andy and Zack that on the days we have salmon or another omega-3 rich fish, we can't take our fish oil pills because then we might get *too many* healthful fatty acids. As I say this, my eyes are soft and dewy and my heart is full of tender love for them because I know full well how hard it is to keep track of all this information. They ignore me.

When next in our freezing lesson I read about trimming deer, moose, antelope, and other large game and removing the bloodshot meat before freezing, I balk. No matter how crazy Zack thinks I am, there will be no digging for bullet shells within a felled animal's flesh, or removing entrails or heads from carcasses. The earth's well-being notwithstanding, this is a no.

CONVENIENCE, BUT AT WHAT PRICE?

For best results, foods need to be tightly sealed in moisture-resistant materials and then quickly frozen to zero degrees or below. In other words, to move forward with step 8, we're going to

Bottles & Sippy Cups
. . . .
For clean water bottles and sippy cups, go to
www.kleankanteen.com.

need to buy special freezer paper, heavy-duty aluminum foil, and freezer bags. What this says to us is that freezing requires lots of wasteful, environmentally unfriendly packing material, so now would be the time to make an investment in reusable, recyclable containers. Happily, there are lots of colors, shapes, and sizes to choose from, and they're all so pretty.

Plus, unlike past pig- and fish-related adventures, I know Zack and Maya will be up for this because they both love shopping at Target. Once I do a little more reading, though, I realize there are a few issues to consider before investing in all new containers, which brings us to step 9 of our makeover: the toxic plastics issue. I didn't see this one coming, and true, plastic isn't technically food, but, I learn, most of us probably ingest enough of it that it might as well be considered a part of our diets.

According to the environmental advocacy group Environment California, many soft plastics contain phthalates, "chemicals that have been linked to premature birth, reproductive defects, early onset of puberty in girls, and reduced sperm quality in adult males," whereas many hard plastics contain bisphenol A (BPA), "a hormone-disrupting chemical linked to Down's syndrome, early onset of puberty, obesity, hyperactivity, and breast and prostate cancer." The safety of both sippy cups and baby bottles is called into question.

Sippy cups and baby bottles might leach poisonous chemicals?

Environment California goes on to specify that a number 1, 2, or 5 in the recycling triangle on the bottom of bottles and food containers signifies a safe plastic, whereas the Environmental Working Group (EWG) says that number 4 is safe but number 5 is not. This is starting to remind me of Zack's math homework, which, while he's only in the fifth grade, is already too hard for me. "Mom, can you help me with — " Zack will start, and then, remembering, he'll add, "Oh right. I have to wait until Dad gets home."

That all-family shopping trip is looking less likely by the minute. Then, to make the already disquieting toxics issue a little worse, EWG adds that the amount of BPA found in canned food in this country is a danger, though at least Japanese industries have voluntarily reduced the use of it, and the food industry in the United Kingdom is considering doing the same, showing that at least some countries are paying attention.

But until there's either legislation passed or American companies are voluntarily making changes in production, which based on American corporations' other voluntary adaptations for the common good won't be anytime this century, we'll try to reduce the amount of canned foods we serve, although what will Maya eat if we stop serving her canned beans? French fries, white bread, and bacon three times a day?

EWG offers a number of practical suggestions on how to reduce the amount of various chemical pollutants we ingest: eat fewer processed foods; eat organic produce; don't microwave food in plastic containers but rather in glass or ceramics; use a water filter; eat fewer meat and dairy products; and choose fish from the fish lists, especially avoiding canned tuna. Thanks to our makeover we're already on track with most of this, but it's still good to see it all in print. I would also add (somewhat bitterly) use dried, not canned, beans.

Of course, there are those like the Plastics Division of the American Chemistry Council who say that food-grade plastics are safe. But in March 2007, EWG released a report about BPA saying, "Few chemicals have been found to consistently display such a diverse range of harm at such low doses."

Which means we're calling off the trip to Target. We'll also be overwrapping the glass storage containers we already have with heavy-duty foil, and recycling our hard plastic number 7 water bottles and replacing them with stainless steel bottles. We'll have to remember to label and date all frozen products, so while we're in shopping mode, buying more *glass* containers and *stainless steel* water bottles, we'll need some masking tape too.

We might also need a vacuum packager. We've seen one featured on infomercials but never gave it a second thought until a friend raved about it; the Web site for one brand tells us we can save more than six hundred dollars a year on food that otherwise would have gone to waste. I'm not sure how they came up with that figure, but at least it's comforting to know we're not alone when we end up needlessly throwing out food.

When he hears I'm researching vacuum packagers, Zack's face lights up. "I have a lot of other recommendations," he says enthusiastically. "Like a power juicer. You don't have to peel or cut anything!" We're not getting a juicer, I tell him, or probably a vacuum packager either — who needs yet another appliance that won't fit on our counter, especially one that uses so much plastic?

BACK TO THE FUTURE

It's not all about modern conveniences, I tell Zack. In fact, it's time for our trip to Plimoth Plantation, a seventeenth-century living history museum in Plymouth, Massachusetts. We're going there for an afternoon of authentic hearth cooking. I'm hoping that a little temporary time travel will show the kids how people managed when they didn't have refrigeration and the kitchen gadgets Zack covets. Not to mention what it was like to be locavores by necessity, not choice.

The idea had originally occurred to me during last February's challenging experiment with locavorism, when Zack had pulled a slightly imperfect apple from the fridge — it had been sliced into the day before — and said, "That's *disgusting*!"

"Just cut the brown part off and it'll be fine," I told him reasonably. He shook his head and grabbed an orange. I'd wanted to take the kids to the museum right after this happened, but Kathleen Curtin, the museum's colonial food historian, seemed resistant. "It's really cold in the house in winter," she'd written. We'd have to wait.

It felt like spring would never come, but after months of anticipation, the big day finally arrives and we're wakened at 5 a.m. by winds so fierce the sound is like ocean waves crashing against our house. The forecast calls for a nor'easter, complete with flood warnings, storm surges, and wind gusts up to 55 mph; according to a "special weather statement" put out by Weather.com, it is "a potentially dangerous situation." We're headed straight for the coastal town of Plymouth. Obviously if we'd wanted good weather for our cooking adventure, we should have done this back in January, when it was 70 degrees and sunny.

"Mom, tell me we're not going in this storm," Zack says.

"We're going. In the seventeenth century . . ."

Zack: "I don't care about the seventeenth century. Dude, we won't even make it there." But when he realizes we're not canceling our trip, he decides to get into the spirit of the day. "Mommy," he asks sweetly, "did they whip people in the old days? Because if anyone gets close to me — " and here he grins and pats his belt, which has hard metal studs on it. So now he's itching to get into it with a colonial role player?

We also managed to convince our friends Ruth and Andrew to join us, along with their kids Susanna, eleven; Jordan, eight; and Abby, five. As our departure time approaches and the rain is still coming down in sheets, the stress level in the house increases: Andy is getting a little terse with me, and I'm getting a little rude with him, until I finally say that he doesn't even have to *come* to Plimoth Plantation if he doesn't want to. "Maybe you should just get out of here," I say callously, but then, in a halfhearted attempt to soften the attack, add, "I mean, why don't you go get yourself a cup of coffee."

Once I realize I've gone too far, I quickly apologize. It only takes us a minute to make up, and then, knowing we're back on track, I can't help myself: I ask Andy if he's taken his vitamins. "Yeah," he answers sadly, "but I didn't take any antidepressants."

Right before we leave home, I call Kathleen to check in and she tells me the electricity in the village has gone out owing to the storms but that we don't need it anyway. "It was their own fault they didn't have electricity," Zack says in response to this news.

"Oh? Why is that?"

"They could have discovered it if they'd wanted," he goes on. "They weren't stupid. All it took was a kite and a key." So far, this experience isn't affecting Zack in quite the way I hoped it would.

Soon enough we're on the road in our respective "low-profile vehicles" — that is, the ones that won't get treacherously blown around by the gale-force winds. Ruth and I are in the car with Abby and Maya, and Andrew and Andy have the three older kids in the frybrid ahead of us. As experienced mothers, we've brought along provisions for the ride, although raw carrot sticks and broccoli aren't really cutting it with the girls. That's when we have to whip out the "natural" fish-shaped crackers that Andy had thrown into my bag at the last minute. For Ruth and me, I've brought thermoses of curried squash soup, which we both savor and spill.

A few minutes into our drive Maya says she doesn't feel well, and I turn around to see blue lips grimly pursed together in a gray face, setting off a frantic search for a plastic bag or container, "just in case." Maybe snacks weren't such a good idea, whether healthy or not. But in the end, we make it to Plimoth Plantation incident-free, by which time the winds have died down and the rain has stopped. Our luck has clearly changed.

We pull into the parking lot and take a moment to regroup and hand out ham sandwiches; we want the kids to be hungry for their colonial meal but not too hungry. We don't linger for long, though, because we're all anxious to get inside the museum. There's something innately appealing about Plimoth Plantation. With the ocean in the background, the English village and its timber-framed houses, each with its own garden and livestock, is picturesque. You have to be in the mood for the costumed role players, though; if you mistakenly ask about kids, for instance, the "villager" answering you will talk about baby goats. There are no role players, only indigenous staff members, at the Wampanoag homesite set by the Eel River, which comes as a relief to those of us older than eleven.

HOME WORK

Months earlier, when Kathleen and I had first gone over the details of our workshop, she had written in an e-mail, "For the cooking project we can go with accurate seasonal foods (bacon,

salt fish, fresh herring, dried corn, dried peas are all very likely)
or go with a (bit) more kid-friendly menu (turkey or chicken for
the protein, pancakes — all less likely but still within the realm of
possibility). Depends on how authentic you want to go." The answer was clear. Why go to all this trouble and then serve the kids
something as delicious as *turkey*? We want them to suff— that is,
learn just how lucky they really are.

Life was arduous hundreds of years ago; as Sandra Oliver writes
in *Food in Colonial and Federal America,* "Settlers built homes
and barns from timber they cut themselves, cleared land and grew
their own food, spun their own flax and wool, wove their cloth
and sewed clothing, churned their own butter, made their own
cheese, and baked bread from the grains they raised." Where'd
they find the time to ferry their kids to all their after-school clubs
and programs?

The reproduction house where we'll be cooking is outside the
English village. It's about the size of our (small) TV room, dark,
cramped, smoky, and cold. It has a dirt floor and a fire blazing in
the huge, freestanding fireplace that serves as a light, heat, and
cooking source all in one. Kathleen tells us that up to nine people
would have lived here; there would have been a sleeping loft too,
as if that would have made a difference.

We're kind of surprised to learn that there were indeed some
spices and sugar in the early seventeenth-century colonial diet,
along with what the colonists grew or produced for themselves:
butter, cream, and milk; eggs and fish and meat; and fresh fruits
and vegetables in season. Still, the diet was monotonous and varied more from season to season than it did day to day, or even
week to week.

In other words, while people had sugar and spices, they used them sparingly. Kathleen tells us that in the seventeenth century, people ate about a pound of sugar per year, whereas today in America the average is 130 pounds. The colonial English settlers weren't big on greens, she adds; vegetables were often just used as a sauce for meat.

Zack: "See Mom? There were no vegetarians."

Me: "See Zack? They only ate seasonally and locally."

But families did eat their midday meal together, just as we'll be doing in a couple hours. True, we'll be in the dark and it's super smoky in here and there are too many people crowded around this one small table with not enough chairs so the adults will be standing up, but that's all authentic too. Although I bet the adults got to sit at the table way back when.

If we'd come in summer, we might be feasting on sweet berries and fresh fish, but since we're here in spring (though it feels like late fall, and thank God we didn't come in February), our historically accurate, mid-April colonial New England menu includes pease pottage, or whole dried peas cooked with bacon and a tiny bit of salt; dried salt cod, which will be deboned by the kids, then cooked with dried ginger and fresh onions; and corn pudding, or dried corn soaked in milk and cooked with eggs, ginger, nutmeg, currants, and a little sugar, then squished into what Kathleen charmingly calls "guts of a pig" to make a type of boiled sausage.

Kathleen has already presoaked the peas, salt cod, and corn. Within minutes of our arrival the kids are hard at work chopping bacon, smashing spices, scraping sugar off the sugar cone, cutting onions, and stirring the pot of "pease" in the fireplace. There is a sense of purpose and focus among the five children, which, though we know it will be fleeting, is impressive nonetheless. Kathleen seamlessly gives directions, tends the fire, chops and cooks, answering questions all the while. We're in the hands of an education master, which makes the experience seem almost easy, at least to some of us.

Fifteen minutes later Maya and Abby have bailed and are playing on the house's one bed. A relaxed Ruth is in there with them, reclining on a pillow and pulling the curtain closed. Next to drop: Zack, who mumbles that he's not feeling well as he books out of the house just after he's blown open the balloonlike pig intestines and squeezed some of the squishy corn pudding mixture in. Jordan follows soon after. By now the twenty-first century is looking better than ever.

Zack returns a little while later to check on the food but leaves again right away, saying the smoke is too much for him. Once he's gone I comment that if the smoke is bugging him that much, then four hundred years ago he might have died. Kathleen replies, "Well, probably." I change the subject.

IT DOESN'T TASTE TOO MUCH LIKE FEET

An hour after we've arrived, all the kids except Susanna are playing with historical games outside the house. Meanwhile, Susanna is pure focus, even willing to work with the nasty-smelling salt cod. Without her, we might have gone hungry today. Well, without her and our own secret stash; as Maya points out, "It's good that we brought our own snacks." Yes, although I later realize that one bright orange "natural" fish-type cracker is probably still swimming on the dirt floor of this perfect reproduction antique house.

With Kathleen at the helm, all three incredibly labor-intensive seventeenth-century dishes end up ready just past 2 p.m. The meal has taken about an hour and a half to prepare. It is so dark in here we can barely see what we're eating. "This is why people ate during the day," Kathleen explains. It's also freezing. "If kids complained about being cold, their mom probably told them to work a little harder." What happened if moms complained about the cold?

"So whaddya think?" Kathleen asks genially once everyone's been served. "You like the pease porridge?" Surprisingly, pretty much everyone does, even Maya; that's because it's really just like a thick, bland pea soup. The fish isn't a crowd pleaser, though; someone unidentifiable in the dark sums it up nicely when he says, "The fish doesn't taste *too* much like feet." But the pudding is okay — a little sweet, a little flavorful — still, not great. There's also a corn-bread "loaf" that's basically a hard, impossibly crunchy discus made from the equivalent of popcorn kernels. "Mmm," Zack says when he first bites into it, "I think I chipped a tooth." When we see that by meal's end the ten of us have eaten almost the whole circle, we know that a mere two hours into our date with history, we're already a little desperate.

When it's time to do the dishes, Zack once again bows out, saying, "I did the least amount of cooking, so I should do the least cleaning up." Naturally this logic meets with universal resistance, so then he takes a different, more obnoxious approach: "Women would be doing the dishes," he says with a smirk. I look to Kathleen for a denial; gallingly, she confirms that he's right. But then she turns to Zack and adds, "But if you're a *servant*..."

"I'm not a servant," he interrupts. "I'm a *successful businessman*." Then he heads back outside. Once he's gotten his laugh, he comes back in and helps.

If life was difficult for the English four hundred years ago, it's hard to overstate what it was like for the Native people after the Europeans arrived. By 1700, "death from communicable diseases brought by the Europeans had already claimed a large number of

Indians in the East. Disease continued to destroy Indians everywhere the white settlers spread. Many Indians were forcibly driven off their lands, and many more lost their lives in settlers' attacks."

Wanting to learn more about this darker side of colonial history, we wend our way over to the Wampanoag homesite; after having spent two dank, dark hours in the colonial house, the *wetu,* or traditional house, is a revelation: bright and fresh-smelling thanks to two skylights that manage to keep rain out while letting smoke from the fire escape; warm and comfortable because it's insulated and there are animal furs on the benches; and to top it off — or rub it in, depending on your perspective — there's a pot over the fire simmering with duck, hominy, two kinds of beans, wild onion, and wild garlic. "Is this what people would have been eating now, in mid-April?" I ask, somewhat regretfully. "It is," a staff member answers. We don't get a taste, but I'm thinking that if we were ever to return for another historic cooking adventure on a blustery, freezing April day, next time I wouldn't be above begging someone at the Wampanoag homesite to take us in.

It's 5 p.m. when we're done with our museum visit, and even though it's been a food-centric day everyone's hungry again. Andrew suggests we take the kids out to eat in nearby downtown Plymouth. We end up at the most horrific tourist seafood spot imaginable, one where a server comes by the table to do stupid lobster tricks ("Want to see Larry the lobster go to sleep?" she asks before rubbing the poor beast's back until it goes limp); another server overtly uses the hard sell to pump up the bill and then "forgets" to mention she's already added in the tip at the end; and we have to tell Zack that we're sorry, but no he can't get the clean, healthy haddock because it has probably been fished in an unsustainable manner.

The fish fiasco also reared its ugly head back at Plimoth Plantation, when Kathleen had told us we'd have to use salt cod because
the local herring fishery has been banned by the state owing to
dwindling stocks. Couldn't all these seafood problems have stayed
within the safe confines of chapter 5? We're supposed to be focusing on Native and colonial life today.

After we're done eating, Maya says hers has been "the yummi-
est dinner ever," and could she get the rest of her (greasy) fried
clams and (flaccid) french fries to go.

"I probably should have learned a lesson," Zack pipes up, "and
I should probably be feeling grateful for all we have, but instead
I just think how much life sucked long ago." I have to agree, although, truthfully, I'd take pease pottage over Maya's nasty fried
clams any day. By the time we leave the restaurant, the seventeenth
century is looking a little better. Ruth goes even further, saying
that our historic meal had been *delicious*. She's not even kidding.
But then, Ruth hates to cook, and today she didn't have to.

By the time we get home, we are all exhausted. Thank goodness
our foray into the distant past had only lasted a day, because I'm
not sure how much more realism we could have managed. Andy
and I kiss the kids good night and go downstairs, where we grate-
fully sink onto the soft couch in our warm, comfortable home to
watch a DVD of *The Office*. The credits roll and Andy passes me a
square of fair-trade dark chocolate. If a spring dinner of salt cod,
pease pottage, and corn pudding eaten in a cold, dank one-room
house exemplifies the zenith of local, seasonal, and authentic, I'm
more willing than ever to work on finding a mealtime middle
ground with my family.

Chapter 9

. . . .

If Mama Ain't Happy
(Ain't Nobody Happy)

THE ROAD TO WELLVILLE

A couple days after we get home from Plimoth Plantation, Maya requests a peanut butter and jelly sandwich for lunch. We have hearty multigrain on hand, and I think, Hey, I bet if I don't say anything about the bread, she will eat this sandwich and love it. It's worth a try.

Maya takes a bite of her sandwich, wrinkles her nose, and says, "I don't like this bread. Can I lick the stuff off from inside?" Yes, I wearily reply. You may.

Okay, so maybe I'm wrong. Maybe we're all doomed to be at odds with each other until Maya, now almost six, leaves for college in twelve years. But we're so close to the end of this makeover; we can't stop now. Instead, we will tackle the final challenge: step 10, whole grains. This could very well be the most difficult transformation of all, because it will require replacing light, sweet, pretty white carbs with denser, chewier, uglier ones. But it's also a critically important step, because bad carbs are the mainstay of most childhood diets.

I've read about the glycemic load before, but that doesn't mean the information has ever sunk in. My nonscientific eyes glaze over when they come across dreary words like sucrose, glucose, and fructose. But with renewed purpose, and knowing that the end is in sight, I hip-check my less scholarly side out of the way and crack open a few more books.

The glycemic load, I read, is a way of quantifying how quickly food that contains carbohydrates — starch or sugars — can raise blood sugar levels in the body. In this case, higher is not better. A glycemic load of under 10 is considered low, so based on a chart in Walter Willett's *Eat, Drink and Be Healthy* whole wheat bread boasts a mere 9, whereas pancakes ring in with an outrageously high glycemic load of 46. White rice, at 23, is higher than jellybeans, 22. And according to the Harvard Medical School, the average baked russet potato has a whopping glycemic load of 26. "Potatoes should be an occasional food eaten in modest amounts, not a daily vegetable," Willett writes. "The venerable baked potato increases blood sugar and insulin levels nearly as fast as pure table sugar."

He's comparing potatoes to sugar?

Come to think of it, this glycemic load thing might be going one step too far. Yes, we know it has an impact on heart disease and diabetes, but thankfully, none of us has either of those. As for weight, which it also affects, we're all out of the woods there too, at least this month. So why should the four of us care about this anyway?

Walter Willett again: "Recent research suggests that the excess blood sugar and insulin that come from eating a high-glycemic diet contribute to other chronic conditions besides heart disease and diabetes. These include breast cancer, colon cancer, and polycystic ovary syndrome." Colon cancer? Breast cancer? Is he kidding? Why didn't anyone tell us? Okay, all right, so they did. But this time, it's sinking in. I guess that, unpleasant as it is, step 10 is here to stay.

THE CUPCAKE CRISIS

I see the mind-boggling power of carbs on Andy's birthday, when Maya's been invited to attend a small party at the office. I pull up to the building to drop her off. Sue is waiting on the steps since Andy's still on the road for work. Maya jumps out of the car and darts off. Sue and I are chatting through the car window when we realize Maya's not in the foyer. "I'd better go get her," Sue says. I nod and then start driving back to school, where I left Zack playing football with his friends.

About thirty seconds later, my cell phone rings. I can see from the caller ID that it's Sue, but when I open my phone there's no reception. Sue has never called me right after I've dropped Maya off, and this gives me a bad feeling, so as I drive toward the school to find Zack, I keep redialing the office. The call won't go through. Cursing the phone, my heart racing, I turn back toward the office, figuring Zack will be fine for a few more minutes; I finally get through to Sue just as I pull up in front of the building.

"I saw that you called," I say quickly when she answers. "Everything okay?"

"Mmm, not really," she says, trying to sound casual. "Maya caught her finger in the door."

"Is she all right? Should I come up?"

"I think you'd better," she tells me. I leap out of the car and fly up the stairs. When I get to the third-floor office a minute later, I find Maya sitting at Sue's desk, her finger tightly wrapped in a paper towel. Andy's officemate Chip is there, and I see that his hand is covered in blood, but while Maya's eyes are red from crying, she's calm now so I figure it can't be too bad. I pull back the corner of the paper, then immediately put it back, turn away, and lean over a nearby table for support. It's the worst injury I've ever seen.

Meanwhile, Maya is still sitting quietly in the chair. I ask her what happened and she explains that she'd pulled open the propped-open front door to the building and raced up three flights of stairs to the office, opening the heavy door and then watching as it closed on the middle finger of her right hand. She's so self-possessed I'm wondering if she could be in shock, so as a test I ask if she wants one of the strawberries meant for the birthday party. She sniffs, frowns, and nods, carefully reaching for it with her unhurt left hand. She takes a delicate nibble. In other words, she seems all right, not to mention heartbreakingly endearing. Andy arrives, and we decide he'll take Maya to Children's Hospital and I'll go pick up Zack.

A couple hours later, Andy calls from the emergency room. Maya, he says, is fine, although her finger is not. Later we'll find out it's broken. But during the entire five-hour ordeal of getting poked, prodded, stuck with gigantic needles, X-rayed, and stitched, she remains a serene, tear-free Zen master. The hand specialist who was called in told Maya she's never met such a brave five-year-old. By the time Andy and Maya leave the hospital, she hasn't eaten anything since lunch nine hours earlier except that one strawberry. We marvel at her strength.

When they get home from the hospital at 8:30 p.m., Maya sees the cupcakes with chocolate frosting and rainbow sprinkles sitting on the dining room table that our neighbor brought over for Andy. We tell her she can have one the next day and she nods.

But the acquiescence only lasts until she is finally upstairs and in her pajamas at 9:30 p.m., two full hours past her bedtime, and she says she "really wants a cupcake." When we gently tell her we're sorry but she has to wait until tomorrow, she bursts into great big sobs for the first time since she broke her finger. And no, this isn't the stress of the day catching up with her; she is crying over cupcakes.

STOCKING UP

With her three middle fingers wrapped in bright red gauze, Maya's actually kind of excited to go to school and be a celebrity. We remind her that she can take a cupcake in today's lunch box ("Yes, Zack, you can have one too"); she wants two.

The next weekend we head to the store, in search of ingredients to use in a cooking marathon designed to prove to the kids how wonderful whole grains taste. I go a little wild. I buy flours made from cereal grasses, seeds, and beans, including teff, amaranth, garbanzo, and whole wheat; whole grains like quinoa, bulgur, kasha, barley, and even the dreaded millet; plus a bunch of dried beans, some slivered almonds, dried apricots — even almond and multigrain "nondairy beverages."

I have no idea how I'll use most of this stuff, but I'm on a tear, and I have to admit, it's even kind of exhilarating. The sun is finally out, we've blown sixty bucks on weird ingredients just because I wanted to — right now, life is sweet. Plus, as an interesting side effect, all this shopping is making me hungry for adventure, for new experiences. I know it's hard to believe I could possibly want more than teff, but I think I do.

On the way out of the store, I shake my head. "Buying all of that without a plan was so — " And just as I'm trying to figure out what it was — sublimating? expansive? — Andy warmly interjects, "Spontaneous?" He's either the most supportive husband around, or else he's desperate to soothe the wild woman he sees breaking loose from her chains. Truthfully, he would probably be more concerned if I had gone for the non-fair-trade imported truffles or ultrapremium ice cream, but I think we both know that teff screams out an enduring commitment to family, hearth, and home.

While I'm clearly on a whole grains bender, Andy, Zack, and Maya will be relieved, if not surprised, to learn that even I cringe when I come across a recipe for carrot wheat germ muffins or that I find recipes calling for applesauce instead of butter and sugar worrisome. And it will make things easier if I admit beforehand that making banana apricot nut bread with amaranth, apple juice, and whole wheat flour will end in waste. But if I think of this as an *experiment,* it takes the pressure off.

When we get home, I make peanut butter cookies with teff flour, canola oil, maple syrup, and peanut butter. They come out of the oven, and unable to wait until they cool, I grab one and take a bite. They're kind of crumbly, but they also taste appealingly of both maple syrup and peanut butter, and something else unidentifiable: must be the teff. I think, Hey, these aren't bad! The next day, once both the cookies and I have cooled down, my reaction is more along the lines of, Well, these aren't *terrible.* Finally I have to admit the truth: they're bad.

Undeterred, I give the recipe another try, this time adding an egg, baking them a little less, and, at the last minute, throwing in a small scoop of fair-trade sugar. That can't be so awful, right? And this time, they really are okay. Maya even wants one in her lunch box, and she and her friend Abby both eat them for a snack. Things are looking up.

Not wanting to completely waste the first batch, we give one of the old ones to Roxy. Andy's dad, in town for a visit, protests, "But they're so *grainy.*" Too grainy for a *dog?* Fortunately, Roxy helps me save face by devouring it. "So the new ones are cookies and the old ones are dog biscuits?" I say jokingly.

"Well," says Andy, "it's a fine line." He's not quite with me on step 10, which reminds me: has he gotten a follow-up test for his cholesterol? "Not yet," he grumbles, but then a few days later, after the kids are in bed, he tells me he went to the doctor's office that morning to have blood drawn. Now we just have to wait for the results.

In the meantime, I keep moving forward. I pull out all sorts of cookbooks, lingering over recipes for hearty breads and healthy-ish cookies and quinoa salad — I come up with a plan for everything we bought except the millet, which still brings up feelings about those leaden, funny-tasting muffins from last winter. Maybe over time the memory will fade and we'll be able to cook with it again, but for now it can stay in the pantry as a reminder of what happens when you go too far.

"Does anyone want hot cereal?" I ask brightly a couple mornings after our Whole Foods run. It's Arrowhead Mills Organic 7 Grain Hot Cereal. Other than me, there are no takers, because for now, the rest of them would still rather have toast. I'm sure they'll come around eventually, but the transition could take a while, so I better put my tranquil hat on. The cereal itself requires patience too; it takes a full fifteen minutes to make, and about the same to eat. (Why are healthy whole grains so *chewy*?) I add maple syrup, toasted almond slivers and dried cranberries, but even so, it all feels very seventeenth century. Or as close as any of us hope to feel to our distant past outside of Plimoth Plantation.

A little while after I eat this fibrous, grainy off-white goodness (and why are healthy whole grains so *brown*?), a revelation hits: I don't feel mildly nauseated as usual. This nausea-free morning gets me thinking about how I feel lousy for at least part of the day, almost every day. I wonder: Could it be due, at least in part, to my diet? Thanks to Walter Willet and step 3 of our makeover, I already know we should be eating less dairy, but I usually have cereal with milk for breakfast anyway. Maybe I shouldn't anymore if this is how I feel without it.

Then I realize that maybe this is actually because of the whole grain cereal itself. I remember reading that foods with a low glycemic load promote a gradual, rather than quick, increase in blood sugar, thereby reducing the chance that it will drop too low, too quickly. Wanting to know more, I go to Medline Plus, a medical encyclopedia sponsored by the U.S. National Library of Medicine and the National Institutes of Health. It says that symptoms of hypoglycemia, or low blood sugar, include "fatigue, general discomfort, uneasiness, nervousness, irritability or even aggression; trembling, headache, hunger, cold sweats, rapid heart rate, confusion, sleeping difficulty, paleness, muscle pain, memory loss, palpitations, hallucinations and dizziness."

Fatigue? Muscle pain? *Irritability or even aggression?* I just attributed all of this to motherhood.

"In the longer term," Medline tells me soothingly, "you may need to modify your diet so that you get glucose into your body more evenly throughout the day. Small, frequent meals with complex carbohydrates, fiber, and fat and avoiding simple sugars, alcohol, and fruit juice may be recommended."

So I should probably be more like the kids and start snacking? Funnily, also like the kids, my first instinct is to celebrate with some cookies or cake (or beer!), but then, remembering what this is all about, instead I grab a midmorning banana with a spoonful of peanut butter; a handful of nuts in the afternoon; and even, one decadent day, a whole grain berry muffin with toasted walnuts in which the butter's been replaced with applesauce and buttermilk. It is surprisingly good.

What's more, I feel noticeably better on the very first day I start eating (high fiber, healthy) snacks between meals. Now that I feel less fatigued and I understand the adverse affects bad carbs can have on all of us, I'm a convert, and while everyone else isn't embracing this step as ecstatically as I am, there's no doubt that from now on, we'll all be eating more whole grains and fewer bad carbs. It will be much easier to follow through on this if we leave the kids at home when we go shopping, though, because children seem genetically programmed to campaign for simple sugars, although that fifteen-billion-dollar junk-food marketing budget might have something to do with it too.

SOMETHING NEW

Back in winter, when I needed it most, I canceled a coffee date with my artsy, funny, wild friend Beck — "Too much work," I'd said, all harried and stressed, and in response she sent me a Harvard study saying, "The more friends women have, the less likely they are to develop physical impairments as they age, and the more likely they are to be leading a joyful life." Got it. I'll never cancel with Beck again.

Instead, I'll invite her to my party — a Girls, Grains, and Greens potluck at my house. I'm having it to celebrate friendship, whole grains, and the search for something ineffable but new. (Of course Beck can't make it; she's working.) I tell my guests they can choose one of four grains — barley, quinoa, bulgur, or spelt — or else something green, although there is no broccoli or lettuce allowed, because most of us have enough of those in our lives already. I can help them find a recipe or they can find their own, but the price of admission is one dish — unless, that is, they're too busy and can't deal, in which case they're welcome to come empty-handed.

I start to doubt whether this party was the best idea when one friend replies that though she's looking forward to it, she wishes she'd been invited for the dessert potluck, and another asks when I'll be hosting the Chicks 'n' Chocolate bash. My worries increase when my friend Claire asks plaintively, "Do we *have* to branch out? Can't we just stay limited?" Then Ruth tells me she's had spelt pasta on her shelf for months; she just hasn't used it for a family dinner yet. Why? Because it's already hard enough to feed her family of five without adding *spelt* into the mix. *"Don't mess with my routine,"* Ruth jokes. I see that I'm not the only mom who gets these big ideas — imagine, spelt pasta — but then backs down and pulls out the white stuff when push comes to shove and there are hungry children afoot.

In other words, I've stressed a lot of people out with this party idea. I'd say I'm sorry, but I'm not. Instead, I'm glad to know I'm not the only one who's so done in by the daily chaos that adding a new ingredient into the regular meal rotation almost feels like an assault. And even though it's hard when someone you thought was a friend asks you to think about bulgur and barley, it's got to be good for us in more ways than one — and not just because a varied diet means we'll be eating more key nutrients. I can't be the only married mother of two in this town who craves a change of pace. Then Ruth says actually she'd be happy to bring a spelt dish because then she can try it risk-free. That's exactly the point of this dinner. I can say that in my case, just seeing a can of chipotles and a bag of tomatilloes on the counter gives me a little thrill.

A LOUSY WEEK

The party is scheduled for a Wednesday night; by the Monday morning before I'm already feeling like it's a lot of work to put together a dinner for twenty-five people, even if it is just potluck. Of course, that's before the call comes in from the school nurse early Monday afternoon. (Calls from the school nurse have almost become de rigueur lately.) "It's nothing serious," she reassures me, but she speaks not the truth, because the reason I need to pick Maya up early from school this time? Lice.

Anyone who's ever dealt with lice will understand the gravity of this situation. No, lice aren't dangerous, and no, they can't make you sick, although if you search the Internet long enough, you can easily find sites that dispute both these reassuring claims. But *Pediculus humanus capitis* have evolved in such a way that they can live long and prosperous lives amid human heads. They're as tenacious as cockroaches, and it takes many, many hours and extreme vigilance to get rid of them. The most common doctor-recommended treatment is to put pesticides on your child's head. I don't think so. Flustered, I tell my sister-in-law what we're dealing with, and in return she gives me a haunting report of three bouts of lice within three months in her home a few years ago. "It was hell," she tells me unnervingly.

When I pick Maya up from school ten minutes later, the nurse tells me she'll check Zack before the end of the day too — his hair is so long that he often gets mistaken for a girl, which makes Andy and me laugh because Zack would make one sorry girl — so when I don't get another call that day I feel hopeful. Until he gets home from a friend's house and I find out that she didn't check him after all. And yes, of *course* he has nits. I see an actual live bug scurrying around the roots of his hair. As if that weren't enough trauma, the next morning, I join the fallen ones. Someone later asks me, "Weren't you itchy?" Well yeah, but who has time to notice itchy?

Let me just say this: Preparing for a party on a weeknight is daunting. Lice infestations on three of four family members is daunting. But the two together could almost take a woman down, especially when they come on the heels of a few months of illness, a broken finger, one canine stroke, and a New England winter. Plus, the minivan brake light is broken. The frybrid needs work done and there are only two people in Boston who can fix it. Maya's birthday is next week; her finger still needs weekly checks at the hospital; and school is about to end, signaling the beginning of a slew of end-of-year events.

The next morning, energized by both purpose and panic, I spring into action. My party is scheduled for the next day, but lice notwithstanding, the show must go on. I am determined not to cancel. I resolutely delouse children in the bathroom, and get down to business making sure we won't inflict this plague on anyone else. Everyone is banished from all upholstered furniture until after the party; the laundry marathon begins apace; and I put in a desperate call to a professional nitpicker — yes, there really is such a thing — which, based on her hourly rate, might be my next career move. The pros recommend throwing pillows in the dryer for twenty minutes; I throw them in the dryer for three to four times that long — twice — then hide them in a corner of my office. Couches should be vacuumed or gone over with a lint brush; mine are vacuumed twice, then gone over with a lint brush five or six times. Lice can live for only twenty-four hours if they're not hunkered down in a person's scalp; my upholstered couches and chair will not even be touched by jeans-covered tushies for two days before my guests arrive. Times like this are when mild OCD seems like a sign of good character.

A few other things we learn: "It's just dandruff" can be the good news. We also now know from experience that we are in fact descended from apes, and I realize that Andy might actually belong to a different species altogether when he's conducting a lice-check on me while the kids are at school and he suddenly leans down and bites my neck. "What the hell are you doing?" I cry out, to which he replies, "Don't be looking all *necky* like that." Seriously, the man is unstoppable. Except, I stopped him.

On Wednesday at 5:10 p.m., after a truly frenzied forty-eight hours, Andy is getting ready to whisk the kids off to the mall when Zack spies the avocado-lime dip with tofu I'd made for the party. It is a gorgeous light green, smooth and luxurious-looking.

"Can you taste the tofu in this?" he asks.

"No, you can't," I answer casually. I can't believe he's asking.

To my shock, he then takes a multigrain chip and dips it in. "This is good," he says with his mouth full, then dips another chip. "This is *really* good."

"Oh yeah?" I say in feigned indifference. "I'm glad you like it." I shrug and turn away as if I hadn't noticed what happened. One more strategy to remember: food is almost always more appealing if it's meant for others.

Five minutes later I find myself sitting alone in an über-clean and quiet house, my nitpicked hair pulled back in a tight French braid, Roxy curled comfortably at my feet. The sky darkens and it starts to rain. I put on a CD, pour myself a glass of Prosecco, and envision my living room filling up with friends in twenty minutes. Despite all the bedlam, I have the wonderful feeling that something important is coming full circle for me. I am regaining something I lost long ago. There's even a sense of repetition somehow — wait, is the CD playing the first track over and over? I forward it to the second song and it happens again. The CD player must be on repeat, but I don't know how to fix it, so for the party there will be no music playing softly in the background.

Just Do It
. . . .
Plan a girls' night, coffee, day, weekend, or whatever out;
it's good for your sanity, skin, and family health. Do it
right this minute.

But sitting in my house, about to see old friends and meet new
ones and share food that's low on the glycemic index, I realize that
I'm not just a nitpicking, dishwashing, calendar-keeping carpool
driver; I need to put myself first like this at least once in a while.
Once I'm rested and well fed, I'll be able to step into my power,
and then, *then* — then the phone rings. It's a recorded message
from Children's Hospital reminding us of Maya's next broken finger appointment. A minute after that, my first guests arrive.

The potluck dinner is, in a word, perfect. The dining-room table
is laden with incredible and unlikely dishes — crispy roasted kale
that's almost like chips; a rich quinoa soup with peanuts; whole
spelt berries with dried fruits that would be great for Thanksgiv-
ing; an Asian-inspired spelt pasta with soy-ginger sauce; earthy
spelt bowties and kasha; minty tabbouleh; herbaceous spaghetti
with green olive and arugula pesto; and banana bread, brownies,
and fudge. (Claire: "Girls need chocolate chips too, right?") By
the end of the night, I see two mothers of toddlers exchange numbers; a journalist hooks up with Kathleen Frith, assistant director
of the Center for Health and the Global Environment at the Harvard Medical School; and I meet a couple new neighbors.

It is exactly what we all needed.

EXEMPLARS, ALWAYS

Soon after the party, the kids and I are in the car on the way home from school when Maya asks, "Zackie, don't you wish we lived in a Strawberry Shortcake world? Then we could climb trees and eat the leaves because they're lollipops."

Much to my surprise, our long-haired preteen who's not exactly into playing pretend anymore answers, "Yeah." He pauses to mull it over for a moment before adding, "It's your fault we don't live in a world like that, Mom."

And though I know he's joking I think, You know what? You're right, though obviously I don't admit this to him. If it weren't for me, the kids would be eating a lot more junk, although candy still wouldn't grow on trees, and they couldn't blame me for that. Of course they'd probably still try.

I once heard a story about Gandhi, a mother, and her little boy. The child wouldn't stop eating sugar, the tale goes, so the mother brought him to see Gandhi. "Bring him back to me in three weeks," the sage one magisterially said to the mother. When she returned, Gandhi told her child not to eat sugar "because it's bad for you."

"Why did you have to wait to tell him *that*?" the (probably ir-ritated) mother asked.

"Because three weeks ago," the master replied, "I was still eat-ing sugar."

This, it seems to me, is wisdom in action. Yes, we adults must be role models for children at all times and in all ways, because the young souls in our care learn about life by watching us. Which means, unfortunately, that Andy and I will have to continue eat-ing candy once Zack and Maya are in bed. Why? Because des-serts not shared with one of the young beggars in the house, not explained or eaten in moderation to set a good example, give us the exhilarating illusion that we're free. Besides, we justify, when we give the kids an inch, they try to take the whole bag of cookies. We've been fighting so much less these days; I've been listening better and trying to lighten up. We'd rather lie than argue.

On the other hand, there's something else to consider: maybe we shouldn't even call it lying anymore but rather "withholding information." After all, some things in life should be adult only, and if Andy and I decide that smooth, luxurious fair-trade burnt sugar truffles taste better when shared with no one but each other, that's our prerogative. We're the parents here.

Then I realize that, call it what you will, there's actually less need to lie, sneak, or otherwise keep information from the kids, because I've been eating far fewer cupcakes and exponentially more whole grains and pumpkin seeds lately. I never would have believed it could happen. But it has, because I've finally figured out that eating better makes me feel better. It's as simple as that. I've also had to acknowledge that if Andy, Zack, and Maya are going to come to this realization too, it needs to be at their own pace.

Just as I arrive at these significant conclusions, something funny happens: people start to come around.

THE ACCIDENTAL STRATEGY

First other adults — one of the school's most popular teachers, Melissa the farmer — start telling the kids not to give Andy and me a hard time about food. Since these adults are far cooler than us, the kids listen.

Then, when we buy a loaf of bread made from quinoa, whole wheat, corn, oats, and rye, topped with flax, pumpkin, and sunflower seeds, we make sure the kids know that Bob from Flora restaurant made it. (Although we don't also mention that the flours are organic. Why push it?) Usually Maya would take one look at this brownish loaf with seeds on top and then shake her head in a declarative no. But now she says, "Bob made it? I wanna taste it." She takes a piece and says, "Mmm, yummy!"

The Bob factor, while obviously very powerful, can only be used sparingly; if we overuse his name, then he might become less influential. So riding on a wave of success, next I try another tactic: I give some to Maya in front of Zack, because there's nothing either of them hates more than being left out of something good. Then I announce, "There's just one tiny end piece left," which is when Zack cuts me off with, "And I have dibs on it."

Purposely creating buzz and competition among the kids is shifty, but it works. Speaking of ruses, when we'd first gotten home from that Whole Foods whole grain shopping binge, I had put the bags with all my exotic ingredients in my office, both so I could keep track of what I'd bought and so I could avoid the usual comments from the peanut gallery. But Maya sniffed them out one morning and asked, "Mommy, what are all these delicious-looking things in your office?"

Teff and garbanzo flour are delicious-looking? I guess forbidden fruit really is tempting no matter what.

"Mommy's experimenting," Andy supportively answered.

"I'm making all sorts of things," I added. "Healthy muffins and cookies — " And then I hastened to clarify: "For myself."

"We can't have any?" asked a disgruntled Zack.

"Of course you can," I answered calmly. "You can try anything you want, but I'm making all this stuff for *myself*." My point wasn't to exclude them; it was to let them know they're no longer under the Mommy microscope.

"That's so *selfish*," Zack replied in an irritated voice.

Bingo.

How could I have forgotten that our children absolutely hate it when their parents have hopes, dreams, and lives that aren't focused entirely on them and that nothing makes them want to get involved more? The best part of all is that for the first time in months, unlike, say, Halloween, or the holiday setback that resulted in the fryer and train cake, or the time of listening when we were wending our way through snackish hell, this wasn't even a scheme. The difference is subtle — it's mostly discernible in slight shifts in tone of voice — but the kids can sense it. In fact, maybe this laid-back approach is better than a middle ground. Lately, I've even been telling them that family happiness might be more important than a healthy diet, but that I really don't want to fight anymore. I mean it — mostly.

So here goes: it's a Wednesday night — a fruit dessert night — and the kids are asking if they can have a brownie for dessert. This is on the same day that Maya has been to the office for a party, and Zack has already had ice cream (long story related to the vexing people problem).

I sigh and say yes, they can have whatever they want.

"Is this that 'I don't want to fight anymore' thing?" Zack asks.

I nod peacefully.

"Mom, us kids don't have any restraint," Zack says, his voice rising. "Say no, Mom, just say no!" He's begging now. "You have to be a mom, Mom, and put up a fight! Without people like you *we'd all be dead*!" Best of all, he's only half-kidding.

I smile serenely and walk away. It's a delicate dance, knowing when to inform and educate, and when to back off. But if executed without anger by an adult who is actually setting a good example by living and eating right, it really seems to work. This becomes evident a few minutes later when I see that while Zack did indeed help himself to a brownie — we only have them in the house because we had friends over for dinner a couple nights ago — he's taken half as much as he usually would. "I don't want to get fat," he says. I just answer, "Oh really?" and drop it. While I'd rather Zack hadn't taken the brownie at all, the fact that he took a much smaller portion clearly shows evolution.

. . . .

At the Table: Take 5

On the menu tonight: organic canned bean and cheese torti-llas with guacamole and rice. This meal has no meat, only a little low-fat organic cheese, and it's rounded out with organic salsa, local lettuce, and greenhouse tomatoes — all in all, another dinner that would pass muster with the nutritionist.

We serve the tortillas with "prepared organic brown rice." "Had to try it," Andy says. It works for me. But what about everyone else?

"Is this healthy rice?" Maya asks suspiciously when I put a spoonful on her plate.

"Why do you ask?" I answer evasively.

"Because it tastes like a grain," she says, wrinkling her nose. That's what it's like for anything off-white around here: guilty until proven innocent. "But," she goes on after taking a bite, "it's still all right." Then she eats the rest.

"Needs salt," Andy mumbles, but once he's tarted it up, he eats it too, as do Zack and I. Things are going along pretty smoothly, in fact, until Zack says wistfully, "I wish we had chips for the salsa."

We do, just not the kind he's talking about: these are multi-grain chips made with brown rice flour, oat fiber, quinoa, and soy flour along with flax, sesame, and sunflower seeds. It's not that these chips are healthy — like any snack food, they're relatively high in fat and sodium — but with three grams of fiber per serving, at least they're better than the usual kind.

"That's all we have?" he asks.

"Yeah."

"Okay." And he eats them. Without complaint.

Indeed, slowly but surely, as the kids get used to all the differences around here, we're noticing there are many fewer protests. Best of all, we don't have potato chips in the house, and we haven't for weeks.

Defy the Rules

- *Quit the Clean-Plate Club.* Never force kids to eat everything on their plate. They need to learn how to listen to their bodies so they know when they're full. (And if they don't eat enough and they go to bed hungry once or twice as a result, chances are that the next time they'll remember to eat enough dinner, even if you're not serving chicken nuggets and fries.)

- *Rewrite the kids' menu.* Most kids' menus are a bummer: fries, dogs, burgers. Try to convince kids to order from the appetizer menu, or else share some of your meal or split an adult entrée between siblings. Some restaurants will let you order half plates from the entrée menu.

- *Say no to TV dinners.* Watching television while eating can lead to overeating or what's now called mindless eating. Don't allow kids to eat while watching TV, playing, or listening to stories. Unless you have to, that is.

Chapter 10

· ·

Where the Ideal Meets the Real

Andy and I are sitting at the dining-room table. A swarm of school papers and bills takes up one half, so we're squeezed into seats near the head — Maya's rightful spot — although Maya herself is in the other room with Zack, watching TV and eating pasta. The four of us are in a rush because we're getting ready for the big end-of-year cakewalk at school, an event that is like musical chairs, only the winners end up with a whole cake. Not surprisingly, the kids can't wait to go, but first, we have to get everyone fed, and since the kids were *starving* before dinner was ready, we quickly boiled up some pasta — at least it was whole wheat — and sent the kids into the other room to eat it. (They cheered.)

Normally we'd just tell them to wait so we could all eat together, even though two hungry kids are, ounce for ounce, unquestionably worse than pasta, even if it had been white. But tonight we're not only in a hurry — God forbid we should be late for possible cake — we're also worn down. It's been an exceptionally difficult few weeks, what with the lice and broken finger, a couple of fevers (Maya and me), along with three sleepless nights because of a stomach bug (Zack). Amazingly, Andy has remained healthy and louse-free throughout.

We were looking forward to this meal, and we wanted to share it with Zack and Maya, because it was going to incorporate so much of what we've learned during the past ten months. But if there's one thing Andy and I have come to understand during the past decade it's this: expect the unexpected, and always have a backup plan.

The kids are still eating in the other room when we finally plate the tilapia, local and organic greens, whole wheat pasta, and spelt. We toast each other with glasses of Smuttynose ale, brewed an hour away in New Hampshire. This is a low-fat, high-fiber, low-glycemic-load, local, fresh, environmentally sound, mostly ethical, utterly modish meal. In terms of applying all we've learned to the real world, it is a total success: our dream dinner.

There's one small problem, though: it's also awful. The tilapia, optimistically cooked in a bath of coconut milk, ginger, and other spices, is pale, wan, and lackluster. The mixture of (local) bok choy and (organic) Swiss chard is bitter, overcooked and mushy. The leftover whole wheat pasta is dry, although I just smother it with jarred vodka sauce and it's fine, but the leftover spelt that Andy decides to try for the first time hasn't been spiced up at all — it's left over from a recipe-testing dish — and it's inedibly dry. Not only is the food a drag, we're not even eating together as a family.

This won't do. We need to finish both our quest and the end of the school year with a dinner that not only combines all we've learned about food and family but that is also festive and tasty. It doesn't have to be fancy — in fact, the simpler the better. As the final act of this particular play, we want to prove to ourselves that the dinner of our dreams is one we can have every night of the week. Or at least a couple nights a week, anyway, when we're all home, and no one's sick. Or fighting.

HAVE SUSTAINABILITY, WILL TRAVEL

Then it occurs to us: the best meal of all would be one eaten with friends. And who better to share this momentous occasion with than Ruth and her crew? She and her husband, Andrew, have invited us down to his family's house in Westport for a few nights after school ends on a Tuesday, which will give us the perfect opportunity to thank them with our new and improved dinner as well as see how someone else's kids react to whole grains and such.

Idyllic Westport, Massachusetts, dates back to the late seventeenth century. There's no town center to speak of, but small shops, restaurants set in historic buildings, and shacklike farm stands dot the winding roads. To this lifelong city dweller, *bucolic* is a synonym for *isolated*, but the school year has been so long, and winter has felt so endless, that even being trapped on the moon for a few days with a friend would be a respite.

Ruth and Andrew, along with Susanna, Jordan, and Abby, spend as much time as they can during the summer at this rambling old farmhouse. They can actually let their kids run around the yard and house without constant supervision. Score one for bucolic.

I pick Maya up from school on her last day of kindergarten, and after a quick stop at home for provisions, we head straight down to Westport, where Ruth, Jordan, and Abby greet us with lemonade and cherries. Susanna is on a trip with her grandmother so she won't be here this week, and the two dads and Zack will join us for the weekend, but until then it's just us moms at the helm. We spend the next few days going to pristine Baker's Beach, the playground, and lounging around the house. Maya and I have never traveled without Zack and Andy before, and we have a sweet time together. Still, we're glad when Friday rolls around and everyone else arrives on the scene. It doesn't hurt that my two guys drive down in the frybrid, because buying this crazy car was one of the most spontaneous, fringiest, sexiest things Andy's done in years.

GONE FISHIN'

Before we left for Westport, I told the kids we'd be preparing a final meal based on all our adventures. "Oh good," Zack said. "We get to use the fryer again?" And that reminded me of one of the most important lessons learned to date: the No Preaching rule. Or rather, the Less Preaching rule, because a mom without at least a little moralizing is like a fish without a bicycle, or something like that. Anyway, the point is that I've decided not to talk to the kids about the theoretical underpinnings of our Saturday night meal any more than I already have. To them, this will be just another dinner.

Once I explained to Zack that the fryer is in the basement and will be staying there, he asked, "Then what are we having?" Well, since we're eating less meat, and since we'll be by the ocean, I told him that we're going to try our hand at catching dinner at a locally renowned fishing spot, Hix Bridge on Westport River.

Fishing was an integral part of growing up in this seaside community a hundred years ago, because the waters were teeming with all sorts of edible delights. Carlton T. Manchester, the author of *Pa and I: Memoirs of a Country Boy at Westport Point,* waxes poetic about catching trout (according to Seafood Watch, these days all the trout in U.S. markets is farmed); shrimp (Oceans Alive: "approximately 90 percent of shrimp sold in the U.S. is imported from countries in Latin America and Southeast Asia, where environmental regulations are lax or nonexistent for both wild fisheries and farms"); oysters (wild eastern oysters contain high levels of PCBs); herring (the Massachusetts herring fishery is closed until 2009); silver-bellied eels (these are given a consumption advisory by Oceans Alive because of mercury, PCBs, and pesticides); swordfish (mercury, overfished); scallops (a Good Alternative choice from Seafood Watch — finally); and clams (two thumbs up; unfortunately no one will eat them but me and Zack).

It's hard to read all these historic fish tales and know we can't follow in the author's footsteps. On the other hand, Carlton and his family only ate what they could catch, hunt, or trade for, so we try to look at it from this perspective and remember to count our blessings. And while we suppose that realistically we probably won't be serving fresh-caught seafood for dinner, once Saturday arrives we pack up our fishing gear, the kids, and a picnic lunch anyway, and head over to Hix Bridge.

It's a perfect day, with blue skies above and verdant green trees surrounding us. Most of us are still unloading the car when we hear Andy shout, "Hey! Cut it out!" He's already down by the river's edge getting out his tackle box when first one, then two rocks come sailing just past his head. It turns out a couple of kids are carelessly throwing them toward the river. It's not an auspicious start to our afternoon.

But rock missiles notwithstanding, we know that we're in the right place at least, because over to our left, and on the dock to our right, we see people hauling in buckets of crabs. The three men standing on the dock have a whole system down: there's the guy holding the net — he's the one with the cigarette dangling from the side of his mouth — and his two cohorts, who throw a long string with raw chicken on it into the water, then slowly pull it back out with crabs attached.

We're surrounded by seasoned locals who are catching enough

crabs for a local, possibly even clean feast. Meanwhile, five minutes into our expedition, lines are tangled; the kids are asking where our crab gear is (who knew?); and Maya and Abby are making Andy nervous by hovering too close to him and his hooks.

But Zack, as yet undaunted, takes his pole and goes up onto the bridge. Half an hour later, scowling and muttering to himself, he returns to our tiny spit of beach empty-handed. We're experiencing the whole range of human emotions out here on the river: hope, frustration, despair — and hunger. It's good that we brought hummus and cucumber slices for lunch (okay, and pizza), along with Andrew's Father's Day present — a kayak — which saves the afternoon. "Fishing is about just enjoying the day, the breeze," Ruth says philosophically; she obviously doesn't equate fishing with actual fish, and unfortunately, we're not going to change this association for her today. It's just lucky we don't have to depend on our outdoorsy skill set for our dinner.

THE DINNER OF OUR DREAMS

While we won't be providing our own fish for dinner, we have a killer menu in place incorporating everything we've learned during our quest; best of all, there's no tilapia anywhere in sight. It looks like this:

Blond sangria made with berries, fruit juices, and sparkling
  wine
Salmon and bacon-wrapped scallops on the grill
Fragrant millet pilaf with cardamom and saffron
Brown basmati rice
Whole grain bread, sliced

Salad of local greens
Chocolate-covered strawberries
Sponge cakes with berries and cream

The sangria combines calcium-added organic orange juice and organic peach and apricot juices with local berries and a squeeze of lime. We make a virgin batch for the kids and then pour ours into glasses along with some Westport Rivers Vineyard sparkling wine. (We're sure the vintner would be horrified, but c'est la vie.) Earlier in the week, Ruth and I had wantonly taken Jordan, Maya, and Abby to the winery, and once we saw they had a kids' play table with LEGOs and crayons, we even more wantonly signed up for a tasting. "We're not on the leisure plan here," I told our host, gesturing to the three kids in the background, and Ruth and I proceeded to while away a delightfully decadent seven minutes speed-tasting wines. At the end, we chose our favorite two selections for our dinner.

It's not always easy to find the answers we need about fish out here in the real world; people don't much like it when you start asking lots of picky questions about what they're selling, even if you do so with a smile. But ask questions we must, because what we see on display is an array of red, to-be-avoided options: local bluefish (mercury); cod, haddock, halibut, sole (overfished or trawl caught); swordfish (mercury); and Atlantic salmon (bad for the environment, PCBs, and other toxins). None of this exactly whets the appetite.

So when I query the shopkeeper about the origin of the scallops, which are one of the few yellow or green list items in the case, he looks at me with a hint of a frown, shrugs, and grunts, "They're from New Bedford." That's pretty near here, and since we're determined to dine on at least one local fish, we buy them. We also get wild sockeye salmon from Alaska, which seems especially insane given that we are literally two miles from the Atlantic Ocean.

Unfortunately, we've run out of frozen bacon from the local farm where we buy our meat these days, and neither Andy nor I had time to head out to there to buy more before we came to Westport. So we compromise with applewood-smoked Niman Ranch bacon. Even though it's been shipped across the country, at least it has supposedly been raised well. Besides, we're using it as a flavoring agent and not as the center of the plate, so that's an accomplishment right there.

As for the grains, we're having organic brown basmati rice since I'd made a batch earlier in the week and Ruth and all three kids had loved it. It's amazing what a little salt can do. But wanting more whole grains on our plate, we're also serving "fragrant millet pilaf," a recipe from *Vegetarian Planet* by Didi Emmons; it contains saffron, cardamom, and orange rind and sounds both exotic and delicious. As an added bonus, it's exciting to think we can reclaim this grain that's high in vitamin B, iron, potassium, magnesium, and zinc, because the last time Andy and I had it was back in December in those sugarless, flourless, joyless millet muffins that tasted like metal. So I've brought some millet from home; it's the same unopened container I've had since our grain-based shopping spree at Whole Foods. Until today, we haven't had the heart to use it.

I'm at the sink busily rinsing lettuce, so Andy starts in on the pilaf. A couple minutes after he's added the grains into the pot, I come over to check it out — it smells great but looks different than I expected. It's quinoa. In addition to millet, I'd also brought quinoa along in case I got inspired to make it.

Once we realize what's happened, and Andy and Andrew see my disappointment, they both lay into me. "It would have been so much better if it had been millet," Andrew says sarcastically before adding, "There's just something *honest* about millet." He then bursts into laughter. Andy points out that the best use of quinoa is probably as a scrabble word. Okay, I say, all right. Enough already. Apparently this wasn't millet's day in the sun after all. We'll get there. Sometime.

Along with our brown basmati rice and our *quinoa* pilaf, and just to round out our newfound focus on whole grains, we also serve slices of multigrain bread. At home we'd put out a little bowl of olive oil, but we forget, so there's nothing on it. No one complains.

The salad contains local lettuce, not-local tomatoes, and a not-local cucumber, but at least the cucumber isn't waxed, and we bought it from a nice woman at a cute farm stand. At this point in the meal prep, we find we have about two extra minutes to play with. We know we can either use this time to make homemade salad dressing that no one but me will appreciate, or else we can use it to help the kids get set up to whip the cream and dip the strawberries in chocolate, which everyone but me cares about, deeply. Bottled dressing it is.

Dessert exhibits mastery of a number of different dietary principles. First of all, our final course features the meal's only dairy; even better, it's in its most exalted form: whipped cream. Second of all, the sponge cakes are small, low fat, and low in calories. And last, dessert mostly consists of gorgeous Westport strawberries and New Jersey blueberries. (Andrew, passing through the kitchen, says, "So strawberries are local and renewable and all that?" I want to answer, That depends, but instead I just smile and nod.)

As for the chocolate, the kids have specifically requested milk and not dark, so we had to give in. Then, we couldn't find any certified fair-trade milk chocolate at any Boston-area store, and by the time we figured out we didn't have any in the house, it was too late to order it online. So instead Andy and I bought Rapunzel Hand in Hand milk chocolate. Hand in Hand is supposedly the company's own fair-trade program, but when I go to its Web site, the link goes to an obsolete URL. Our fingers are crossed that Rapunzel is good for its word.

While the kids are out on the back porch dipping strawberries in melted chocolate and whipping up the cream and sugar, Andrew, Andy, Ruth, and I slip into the living room for a quick toast: to eleven years of friendship and parenting, and to a better world for our children. We raise our glasses, take a sip, and smile; we have shared so many —

"Sorry to interrupt," Zack says as he comes into the room, clearly not sorry at all, "but the cream isn't whipping. We need some help." And just like that, the moment's over.

DIGGING IN

By the time dinner is ready, late afternoon has segued into a gorgeous New England evening, with shadows falling across the lush lawn and a touch of early summer chill in the air. We decide to eat on the back stairs, balancing our plates on our laps. Roxy is frolicking in the yard during dinner. Maya agrees to eat rice, bread, tomato, and bacon, but at least the rice and bread are organic and brown. Then, in the middle of dinner, out of the blue, she says, "I'll taste some of that," and she points to the salmon on my plate.

Not wanting to push my luck, I pass her one tiny flake on my fork. Unbeliveably, she takes a nibble. Well? What does she think?

"It's pretty good," she says.

"Want some more?" I ask.

> *Reminder*
> . . . .
> When fighting the good nutrition fight, keep the faith,
> maintain a sense of humor, and hide the hot fudge as
> needed. Remember, it's not lying; it's having adult time.

"No thank you. Can I have some more bacon?"

At least Jordan loves the salmon; he even asks for seconds. He also has salad, rice, and a bite of the quinoa, which he doesn't really like, and which Zack actually hates, saying, "I will not be having any more of that chinwee stuff." But he devours the scallops with bacon, salmon, and rice. The scallops are especially good tonight, because having learned from past mistakes, this time we par-cooked the bacon in the microwave. The salty, supercrisp bacon is a perfect foil to the sweet, tender mollusks.

Andy then shocks me by calling the quinoa "delicious"; when I ask if he's kidding, since I don't really agree — I bet it would have been better with millet — he says, "What can I say, I like my own cooking." I knew about the trick of getting kids to try something new by having them help prepare it, but I thought it only worked with people under eighteen.

After dinner Andrew comments, "That didn't seem too hard," and Ruth says, "That's because we didn't cook it." But Andrew's right: this dinner for eight wasn't hard to make at all, and it was good to boot. Fait accompli. Andrew then rounds the kids up for a game of croquet while I scurry into the kitchen to dish up dessert. I go heavy on the berries and light on the cream, using the chocolate-covered strawberries as a garnish. These plates are a portrait of restraint and good taste. The perfect ending to our meal.

The combination of the soft cakes, the lightly sweetened whipped cream, and the slightly tart berries is so luscious that I probably shouldn't be surprised when Andrew says, "I fully intend to have another sponge cake after the kids are in bed," and Ruth dreamily wonders aloud, "Can I just not eat anything except this?" I think, People, please. I fully understand the sentiment, but can we keep it under wraps until the small fry are upstairs in bed?

A REVOLUTION IN BABY STEPS

While much of what we've learned hasn't been breaking news, now we see it's actually possible to implement change, even with the kids resisting and Andy down in the basement filtering oil for his car and either Roxy or one of the kids waking us up most nights. Indeed, the four of us have made a lot of incremental adaptations during the course of our makeover, and while they may seem unimpressive taken one by one, in the end they actually add up to something major. As my friend Martha always says, taking baby steps is the key.

Everyone is taking daily(ish) vitamins now, and Zack, Andy, and I are also taking fish oil pills. We buy all our eggs and most of our meat from a local farm, and we finally found a farmer that sells chickens; he even told me that if I can get enough people to sign on, he'll be willing to make deliveries directly to our homes next winter. Local or not, though, we're eating much less meat and dairy lately. We've also been stocking our new freezer with seasonal fruits — strawberries, blueberries — and we're trying to psych ourselves up to start on vegetables too, even though I fear and loathe blanching. I've also decided that beets or no, I'm signing up for the winter CSA again, but this time I'll find a friend to share it with.

We only buy fair-trade chocolate, sugar, coffee, and tea for home use now. Our fish consumption has completely changed thanks to the fish lists. I ordered a couple of stainless steel water bottles for the kids online. We almost always serve whole grain breads and pastas these days, and we're all eating less pizza, brownies, cake, and all the rest. By now I know we'll never eliminate these from our diet entirely, although when push comes to shove, I guess I wouldn't even want to.

Over time, each one of us has also been personally affected by this project in a different way. As Zack puts it one day, "Mom, you have really accomplished something because I won't eat meat out anywhere these days."

"Really?" I ask. "It's not that I don't want meat," he goes on. "It's that I don't want all the stuff that could be in it. Except," he then adds thoughtfully, "for barbecue."

Maya's first moment in the sun came when she allowed that seminal flake of salmon to touch her tongue in Westport; a couple weeks later, without any additional prodding, she gives us an astounding encore by actually eating barramundi for dinner. This is followed a week later by tilapia fish sticks.

My own wondrous transformation comes in two parts: first and most important, learning about whole grains and the glycemic load has changed my life. I have more energy and less muscle pain than I have in years.

To demonstrate the second benefit, which is more incidental but not without an attendant moment of satisfaction, we need to enter Maya's day camp for a moment. It's first thing in the morning, and as I'm dropping her off, I'm surrounded by three adorable six-year-old girls, one of whom is telling me she notices I'm wearing the same outfit I had on yesterday. She's right; that's because I only own three pairs of shorts. The very next day, shamed into it by a first-grader, I go shopping, and I discover I've gone down a size. Weight loss was never one of my goals, but now that it's here, I'll take it.

As for Andy, a letter from the doctor arrives one day when he's at work. I know it's about the follow-up blood work he had done to check on his high cholesterol, so I immediately call him and ask if I can open it; in fact, I'm already sort of ripping the envelope while I'm dialing. When he says yes, I skim over the paper as fast as I can. His lipid panel is "much, much better," the doctor writes, and his hemoglobin is out of the diabetic range.

But some things haven't changed: Andy will never eat vinegar or tomatoes. And we should all probably eat more leafy green veggies, and we need to remember to have the kids brush their teeth in the mornings so Maya doesn't end up with eight fillings too, like Zack. But given where we started, we're doing more than all right.

IT HASN'T BEEN A CAKEWALK, BUT ALMOST

Eating well takes more effort, sacrifice, and expense, but now we've found that the payoffs have been worth it. We've become more of a team. This became clear as we were getting ready to go to the cakewalk up at school after our eminently sustainable but highly unpleasant dinner of tilapia and greens. Before we left home, Zack asked what we should do if he or Maya won a cake. Just as Andy and I were mulling it over, Zack himself came up with a suggestion. "If we win," he said, "we won't have any tonight, but we'll be allowed to take some in our lunches tomorrow." This was so wise and reasonable that we immediately agreed, and while Maya was still hemming and hawing, Zack bent down on his knees so he'd be at her eye level and convinced her to say yes. This put us all in a good mood.

The night only got better for the kids, because an hour after we got to school Zack finally made it to the front of the long line and into the actual cakewalk, where he circled around the chairs to the music, sat down in a numbered chair, and smiled when his number was called out over the microphone. Caught up in the joyful largesse of a man in the winner's circle, he took Maya's hand, walked her over to the awards table, and generously let his sister pick out the cake. She chose a sassy pink number dolled up with a multicolored candy smile and marshmallow cheeks. It hurt me even to see it, but, as promised, there were no arguments or pleas for a taste of it that night; also as promised, there were slices of it in the next day's lunch.

"Don't give up the good in search of the perfect," Ruth advises. She's right, because while nothing will ever be perfect — not our diets, marriage, parenting, or anything else — we've still unquestionably evolved. There's still more work to be done, and we'll always have to work within the confines of family life, but we're unquestionably moving forward, step-by-step and bite-by-bite. Transformation may not arrive at a breakneck speed, but we're making it happen nonetheless, one small but savory forkful at a time.

Tips, Charts, Recipes, and Places to Go

Tips and Charts
· ·

PRODUCE

This list is from the Environmental Working Group. It summarizes which produce is generally lowest in pesticides and which to buy organic (www.foodnews.org):

Dirty Dozen (buy these organic)
Peaches
Apples
Sweet bell peppers
Celery
Nectarines
Strawberries
Cherries
Lettuce
Grapes (imported)
Pears
Spinach
Potatoes

Cleanest Twelve (lowest in pesticides)
Onions
Avocado
Sweet corn (frozen)
Pineapples

Mango
Sweet peas (frozen)
Asparagus
Kiwi
Bananas
Cabbage
Broccoli
Eggplant

VITAMINS AND MINERALS

Recommended Dietary Reference Intakes of Selected Vitamins and Minerals

	1 – 3 years	4 – 8 years	9 – 13 years
Vitamin A (µg/d)	300	400	600
Vitamin C (mg/d)	15	25	45
Vitamin E (mg/d)	6	7	11
Folate (µg/d)	150	200	300
B6 (mg/d)	0.5	0.6	1
B12 (µg/d)	0.9	1.2	1.8
Calcium (mg/d)	500	800	1,300
Iron (mg/d)	7	10	8
Zinc (mg/d)	3	5	8

µg/d = micrograms per day
mg/d = milligrams per day
Source: Reprinted with permission from the National Academies Press,
© 2006, National Academies Press.
Note: To look up other vitamins and minerals, go to www.iom.edu and click on Food
& Nutrition, then on Dietary Reference Intakes. Scroll to the bottom of the page
and click on "To view the table of DRI values, click here." Then download the PDF
document.

   These tables display recommended dietary allowances (RDAs), or "the average daily
dietary intake level sufficient to meet the nutrient requirements of nearly all (97–98
percent) healthy individuals in a group." Calcium is the only exception; those numbers
are not RDAs but rather adequate intakes (AIs). "If sufficient scientific evidence is not
available ... an AI is usually developed ... Lack of data or uncertainty in the data
prevent being able to specify with confidence the percentage of individuals covered
by this intake."

GOOD FOOD SOURCES

The following are reliably good sources of the listed vitamin or mineral—in other words, an average serving will give you a healthy dose of the nutrient. This list was compiled from the National Institutes of Health dietary supplement fact sheet, USDA list of dietary guidelines, and *Feeding Your Child for Lifelong Health* by Susan Roberts and Melvin Heyman. Sources are generally listed in order of predominance.

Good Sources of Iron
Clams and oysters
Lean beef
Lamb
Eggs
Sardines
Fortified cereals
Fortified baby cereals
Lentils
Beans
Blackstrap molasses
Tofu
Spinach and other dark green leafy vegetables
Wheat germ
Fortified breads
Egg noodles
Dried apricots

VITAMINS AND IRON: TOO MUCH OF A GOOD THING

First of all, if your child eats food fortified with lots of vitamins and minerals, as some cereals are, then she doesn't need a multivitamin too.

Furthermore, iron's especially tricky because while too little is harmful, so is too much. Check multivitamin labels for grams of iron and cross-reference it with the table on page 230, taking into account how much red meat and fortified foods your family eats. If your kids regularly eat red meat or fortified foods—say, four to five times a week—they probably don't need supplementary iron. As Drs. Roberts and Heyman write in *Feeding Your Child for Lifelong Health*, "It is almost impossible to get too much iron from regular foods ... But supplements containing only iron should never be given to children unless prescribed by their pediatrician for a specific problem. You should also keep any supplements that contain iron out of children's reach."

Good Sources of Calcium
Milk
Yogurt
Calcium-fortified juice
Cheese
Frozen yogurt
Canned sardines and canned wild salmon, both with bones in (if you're brave enough)
Broccoli, kale, and other dark green vegetables
Tofu

Good Sources of Zinc
Oysters (if you can get anyone to eat them)
Lean beef
Lamb
Turkey
Dark chicken meat
Egg yolk
Yogurt
Milk
Hard cheese
Peanut butter
Fortified cereals
Whole wheat bread
Beans
Yellow wax beans
Peas

Good Sources of Folate (also known as folic acid)
Spinach
Beans
Asparagus
Green peas
Orange juice
Broccoli

Good Sources of B6
Baked potatoes
Bananas
Chickpeas
Oatmeal
Chicken
Beef
Fish
Wheat germ
Prunes

Good Sources of B12
Fish (clams, wild sockeye salmon, farmed rainbow trout)
Beef
Yogurt
Milk
Eggs

Good Sources of Vitamin A and Beta Carotene
Sweet potatoes and winter squash
Carrots
Orange fruits (cantaloupe, apricots, papaya, mango)
Spinach and kale
Milk
Peas
Tomato juice

Good Sources of Vitamin C
Kiwi fruit
Oranges and orange juice
Sweet peppers
Cantaloupe
Broccoli
Strawberries
Tomatoes
Cauliflower
Pineapple
Kale
Mango

Good Sources of Vitamin E
Canola, corn, and sunflower oils
Nuts and seeds
Peanut butter
Avocados
Wheat germ
Carrots
Spinach

Seafood
Fish cards that highlight the pros and cons of consuming various species may be found at the following Web sites:

www.mbayaq.org/cr/seafoodwatch.asp
www.oceansalive.org
www.kidsafeseafood.org
www.blueocean.org/Seafood

It's all too confusing? Try these lists:

Green

The first seven choices are also high in omega-3 fatty acids.

Wild-caught salmon from Alaska (fresh, frozen, and canned)

Barramundi (look for Australis; not available for retail sale in most parts of the country, I'm sorry to say, but that may change soon — go to www.thebetterfish.com)

Sardines

Anchovies

Atlantic herring

Atlantic mackerel (*not* king or Spanish)

Oysters (farmed)

Bay scallops (farmed)

Tilapia (U.S. farmed)

Mussels (farmed)

Tiny salad shrimp

U.S.-farmed crayfish (never seen 'em at any store in Boston)

Catfish (farmed)

Clams (farmed)

Crab (Best is snow, but Jonah and Alaskan king and Dungeness are still okay. There's no doubt that crab is controversial.)

Pacific cod (*not* Atlantic cod)

Calamari/squid

Wild-caught pollock from Alaska

Anything from Henry & Lisa's Natural Seafood (www.ecofish.com)

Arctic char

Red

Chilean seabass/toothfish

Atlantic cod

Atlantic flounder, sole, haddock, hake, halibut

Monkfish

Orange roughy

Farmed salmon (aka Atlantic salmon, ocean-farmed salmon)

Shark
Skate
Red snapper
Grouper
Imported caviar
Swordfish
Tilefish

If you buy fish oil, make sure the label specifies "pharmaceutical grade"; Environmental Defense has information on the safety of fish oil from seventy-five companies on its Web site (go to www.oceansalive.org and click on "Eat Smart"). Oceans Alive also has many other facts and tips on seafood safety, also under "Eat Smart."

BOOKSHELF

If you want to buy one (and only one) book to learn more about food, make it *What to Eat* by Marion Nestle.

Other Great Books
Consuming Kids, by Susan Linn
Eat, Drink and Be Healthy, by Walter Willett
Fast Food Nation, by Eric Schlosser
Feeding Your Child for Lifelong Health, by Susan Roberts and Melvin Heyman
Food Fight: The Citizen's Guide to a Food and Farm Bill, by Daniel Imhoff
Grub: Ideas for an Organic Kitchen, by Anna Lappé and Bryant Terry
The Omnivore's Dilemma, by Michael Pollan
The Way We Eat, by Peter Singer and Jim Mason

OTHER STUFF

The Two Angry Moms have a film and Web site about improving school lunch programs nationally. Amy is an award-winning filmmaker, and as the Web site explains, "Susan has earned herself a reputation as a rabble-rouser with a 'macrobiotic agenda' (NOT!). She's even been banned from her children's school cafeteria." How awesome do these two sound? To learn more, go to their Web site, www.angrymoms.com.

Recipes

"Shh, It Has Tofu in It" Dip
(Adapted from *Vegetarian Planet,* by Didi Emmons)

Zack made this and did a great job, omitting the cilantro at his mom's request. When he was done, he asked, "Do we even have any corn chips?" I wasn't sorry to say we didn't. "We can eat it with crispy kale!" I answered enthusiastically. He wasn't amused.

Makes 1½ cups

> 1 ripe Hass avocado, peeled and pitted
> 3 tablespoons freshly squeezed lime juice (from about 1½ limes)
> ½ cup silken tofu
> 3 tablespoons chopped fresh cilantro
> 1 teaspoon ground coriander
> 1 garlic clove, peeled
> ⅓ cup canola oil
> Salt and freshly ground black pepper

Using a handheld immersion blender or a food processor, combine avocado, lime juice, tofu, cilantro, coriander, and garlic. Blend well. With the blender or processor running, slowly pour in the canola oil. Season with salt and pepper.

Thanksgiving Side Dish

(keep it vague and maybe they'll try some)

(Adapted from *Joy of Cooking*)

When I went to buy whole spelt berries at Whole Foods, much to my surprise they were sold out. A run on spelt berries? Who'd have thought?

My friend Marlissa, who brought this crowd pleaser to the Girls, Grains, and Greens party, writes, "If you soak the spelt berries in water overnight, cooking time is cut in half... I didn't think about doing that until 11:00 a.m. on the day of the party, so I just soaked them for a couple of hours." And everyone loved it.

Serves 4

> 2 cups uncooked spelt berries, soaked overnight (or not)
> 1 gallon salted water
> 2 tablespoons unsalted butter or olive oil
> 1 cup chopped onions
> 2 cups diced mixed dried fruits (such as golden raisins, raisins, cranberries, and cherries)
> 1 cinnamon stick
> 1 cup chicken stock (or vegetable stock or water)
> Salt and freshly ground black pepper
> ½ cup chopped walnuts, pecans, or blanched almonds, toasted

Add the berries to the salted water. Gently simmer, uncovered, until tender but still chewy, at least an hour. (Cooking time will depend on how long — or whether — you soaked them.) Drain and set aside.

Melt the butter in a large pot. Add the onions and cook until golden, about 10 minutes. Add the diced mixed dried fruits. Stir to blend, and then add the cooked spelt berries, cinnamon stick, and chicken stock. Cover and cook, stirring once or twice, over low heat until the flavors are blended, about 10 minutes. Season with salt and pepper. Sprinkle the nuts on top.

Make Kale, Not Cake
(Adapted from Mollie Katzen's *Vegetable Heaven*)

"What are you making?" Maya asks.

Me, thinking fast: "Green crackers!"

Maya, suspiciously: "Oh." A few minutes later, when the kale is done, I pull it out and give the kids each a taste. They then stand by the stove stuffing their faces with kale. Maya has never eaten so much green stuff in her life. Then again, this kale is crackly, crispy, and salty—what's not to like?

As Maya explains, "At first I thought, when you said you were making these *green crackers*"—and here she laughs—"that I wouldn't like them. But I do! They're yum, yum, yummy." Talk about success!

One more thought: If it's very humid when you make these, the kale might lose its crunch all too quickly. You can just crisp it up again in a hot oven.

Makes 2–4 cups (depending on how crispy you like it)

> 1 head curly kale (the stems on dinosaur kale get too tough)
> Olive oil or canola oil cooking spray
> Salt and freshly ground black pepper

Preheat the oven to 350 degrees F.

Wash and dry kale and then chop or tear it into medium-size pieces. Spread it out on a nonstick baking sheet. Spray the kale lightly with oil, and then sprinkle with salt and pepper to taste. Bake 12–15 minutes until light and crunchy (check every few minutes and give pan a little shake to avoid burning).

Blond Sangria

This drink is like a party in a pitcher and it makes us inordinately happy. Be sure to make a virgin batch for any kids hanging around, or else you'll feel like a heel; yes, I speak from experience. We won't make that mistake twice.

Serves 4–6

2 cups apricot juice
3 cups peach juice
¼ cup orange juice
Juice from 1 lime
3 cups white wine
cut-up summer fruits (such as plums, peaches, blueberries, nectarines, or whatever you have around)
¼ cup Triple Sec (optional)

Mix all the ingredients in a large pitcher, pour over ice, enjoy . . .

Even the Kids Love Butternut Squash When It's in This Pie

Just hours after I got an assignment from *Wondertime* magazine to write about winter squash, Maya, then four, (psychically) said, "I want to eat squash more often."

"You do?" I asked, eyes wide.

She nodded emphatically and said, "Yes! I do!"

Naturally I was more than a little surprised by this turn of events, but then I thought about it for a minute and decided to seize the moment.

"We can have more squash!" I told her enthusiastically, at which point we both burst out laughing. Winter squash had suddenly brought so much happiness into our lives! She then helped me bake squash pies until we came up with this recipe, which, amazingly, she and Zack both love, so naturally Andy won't try it.

Serves 8–12

>   1 small (2-pound) butternut squash (about 2 cups mashed)
>   1 tablespoon vegetable oil
>   1 frozen deep-dish pie crust
>   ½ cup light cream
>   ¾ cup sugar
>   1 teaspoon ground cinnamon
>   ½ teaspoon ground ginger (optional)
>   ¼ teaspoon ground allspice (optional)
>   ⅛ teaspoon salt
>   3 large eggs, at room temperature

Preheat the oven to 400 degrees F.

Halve the squash lengthwise, and then scoop out the seeds. Line a baking pan with foil and put the squash in the pan, cut sides up. Rub the cut sides with oil, and bake until very soft, about 1 hour.

Half an hour after you put the squash in the oven, take the pie crust out of the freezer; defrost until soft, 10 to 15 minutes. Have your helper prick the bottom of the crust all over with a fork, then bake it next to the squash until the edges just start to turn brown, 5 to 8 minutes.

Take the squash and pie crust out of the oven and set them on a rack to cool. Turn the oven down to 375 degrees F. When the squash has cooled a bit, help your sous chef scoop the flesh into a blender or the bowl of a food processor. Add the cream, sugar, spices, and eggs. Pulse, scraping down the sides as needed, until smooth.

Put the cooled pie shell on a cookie sheet and pour in squash mixture. Bake until the filling is set and crust is golden brown, 40 to 45 minutes. (After 20 minutes, check the crust; if it's getting too brown, tent a large piece of aluminum foil over the pie while it finishes baking.)

Cool pie 15 minutes before serving. If you want to save it for later, cool it to room temperature (about 2 hours) and then store in the fridge. (Bring the pie back to room temperature before serving.)

Miraculous Fish Sticks with Dipping Sauce

(Adapted from a recipe by Sara Moulton on
Kidsafe Seafood, kidsafeseafood.org)

The almost miraculous news about this recipe is that both kids and Andy ate these. The bad news is, it turns out I despise tilapia no matter how crunchy it may be. But I'd rather go hungry once in a while if it means watching my family eat green-list, Kidsafe-approved fish.

Serves 4 tilapia lovers

    Oil for spraying on cookie sheet
    1 cup all-purpose flour
    1 teaspoon salt
    1 teaspoon garlic powder
    2 teaspoons sweet paprika
    2 cups panko bread crumbs (check labels for trans fats, though,
        and substitute regular bread crumbs as needed)
    1 pound tilapia fillets
    1 cup low-fat milk

Preheat the oven to 425 degrees F.
    Lightly oil a cookie sheet.
    Combine the flour, salt, garlic powder, and paprika in a shallow bowl and mix well. Put the milk in a second bowl and the panko breadcrumbs in a third.
    Cut the fillets into strips, or "fingers" if you will, then rinse them under cold water. Dry the fingers with a paper towel and dip each piece in the flower mixture to coat on all sides, shaking off the excess. Next, dip the pieces in milk, and then in the breadcrumbs, coating well.
    Arrange the fish on the oiled cookie sheet in a single layer, with space between them. Bake in preheated oven for 20 to 25 minutes, turning them halfway through, until they have become extra hard and crunchy, which is the only way they'll get eaten, at least in this house.

Dipping Sauce

Sara provides the following recipe for a dipping sauce. As I started whipping it up, Maya came into the kitchen.

"Whatcha making now?" she asked.

"Sauce for the fish."

"Pee-yuck," she said, and meant it. Zack wouldn't eat it either, but here's the recipe anyway, just in case your people like Russian dressing.

Makes ½ cup

¼ cup low-fat mayonnaise
¼ cup ketchup
2 tablespoons finely chopped dill pickle
1 teaspoon pickle juice
½ teaspoon freshly squeezed lemon juice
Salt

Combine the mayonnaise, ketchup, pickle, pickle juice, and lemon juice in a bowl and stir until smooth. Season with salt to taste.

We Finally Used the Millet Pilaf
(Adapted from *Vegetarian Planet,* by Didi Emmons)

I can't remember where I saw a hulled millet recipe that reminded the reader to "be sure to get hulled millet, not birdseed!" I found that worrisome. But luckily, millet turns out to be pretty good. I can't speak for birdseed. Maya even ate some plain (pre-pilaf) with soy sauce and she "ate it all uu—up." Still, I don't think we'll be making it into muffins anytime soon.

Serves 4

> 1 tablespoon olive oil
> 1 cup minced onions
> 1 cup hulled millet (not quinoa)
> 1 teaspoon ground coriander
> ¼ teaspoon ground cardamom
> 1 pinch saffron threads
> 1 teaspoon salt
> Freshly ground black pepper
> 3 cups chicken stock, plus more as needed
> Kernels from 2 ears corn, or 1⅓ cups frozen
> 1 teaspoon grated orange rind
> 1½ cups chopped tomatoes, fresh or canned (we omitted these
>   on Andy's behalf)
> 2 tablespoons chopped chives or scallions

In a heavy saucepan, heat the oil over medium heat. Add the onions and sauté for 5 minutes, stirring frequently. Add the millet, coriander, and cardamom and sauté for another minute or two, stirring constantly. Add the saffron threads, salt, pepper, and stock. Bring to a boil over high heat; then cover the pan and simmer for 30 minutes.

When the millet has simmered for 30 minutes, add the corn and orange rind. Stir well, cover the pan again, and continue cooking for 5 more minutes.

Stir the tomatoes into the millet. Taste for seasoning, and then spoon the millet pilaf onto plates. Garnish with the chives or scallions.

Bob Sargent's Bean Soup with Just a Little Pig

"I'm making bean soup today!" I tell Maya one morning while we're snuggling on the couch.

"I don't like soup," she says. She's still waking up, I'm sure that's the problem.

"But you love beans!" I reply, ever chipper.

She snarls. Maybe next time I'll just make the soup instead of talking about it beforehand and see how that goes.

Serves 4

2–3 tablespoons extra-virgin olive oil
2 cups diced onions
1 cup diced carrots
1 bunch green Swiss chard, washed and separated into stems and
    leaves; coarsely chop each and keep separate
1 or 2 links chorizo sausage, sliced thinly (yes, I know it's vague)
2 tablespoons minced garlic
Generous pinch of salt
Enough water or vegetable or chicken stock to cover the beans by
    an inch (Bob uses water but says it doesn't matter which you use)
1 pound navy beans, soaked overnight

Heat the oil gently in a 3- or 4-quart soup pot over medium heat. Add the onions, carrots, chard stems, and sausage. Cook until vegetables are slightly softened and fragrant, about 10 minutes. Add garlic and salt, and stir. Pour in the beans and enough water or stock to cover, plus 1 inch. Bring to a boil, then turn the heat down and cook at a lively simmer for 1 to 1½ hours, or until the beans are as soft as you like, adding more liquid as needed. Toss in the chard greens, taste for seasoning, and cook until the greens are wilted. We eat this with garlic bread and salad.

Celeriac Bisque

(Adapted from Epicurious.com)

We served this bisque on a cold winter's night; it was smooth, creamy, and a beautiful off-white. The three of us all had second servings (and at least Maya's pasta was whole wheat). After dinner, I said with a smile, "It's good, right?" Andy nodded, paused, then asked, "But what's for dinner?"

Serves 6–8

> ¼ cup (½ stick) unsalted butter
> 1 cup chopped celery
> ½ cup coarsely chopped shallots (about 3 large shallots)
> 2 pounds celery root (celeriac), peeled, woody parts trimmed and discarded, and cut into ½-inch cubes (about 5½ cups)
> 1 10-ounce russet potato, peeled, and cut into 1-inch pieces
> 5 cups low-salt chicken broth
> 1½ teaspoons minced fresh thyme, plus more for garnish
> ¼ cup light cream
> Salt and freshly ground black pepper

Melt butter in a heavy large pot over medium heat. Add the celery, cover, and cook until slightly softened, about 3 minutes. Add the shallots; sauté uncovered 3 minutes. Stir in celery-root cubes, potato, broth, and thyme. Increase heat to high, and bring to a boil. Reduce the heat to medium-low, cover, and simmer until vegetables are very tender, about 40 minutes. Cool slightly.

Working in batches, transfer soup to blender and puree until smooth. Stir the cream into the soup, and bring to a simmer. Season to taste with salt and pepper. Ladle the soup into bowls. Sprinkle with additional chopped thyme, and serve hot.

Scallops and Bacon

For us New Englanders, scallops are the only relatively clean, sustain-
able-enough, local fish around these days; even ethicist Peter Singer
deems them all right to eat. Plus, they're so sweet and tender that the
three of us love them, and the other one is just happy to find bacon at
dinnertime, even if it's wrapped around fish.

All in all, this one's a winner.

NB: While Seafood Watch considers farmed bay scallops a Best Choice, they're
hard to find and, because they're so small, would be hard to use in this recipe.
Instead, look for diver-caught sea scallops from the Northeast or Canada. Avoid
sea scallops from the mid-Atlantic.

Confusing enough?!

Serves 4

Olive Oil Mixture

3 tablespoons olive oil
2 teaspoons freshly squeezed lemon juice
1 tablespoon chopped fresh chives or other herbs
1 teaspoon salt
Freshly ground black pepper

⅓–½ pounds bacon strips
1 pound scallops (approximately 16), rinsed, dried,
    and tough muscles removed
Bamboo skewers soaked in water for ½ hour

In a small bowl, combine all the ingredients for the olive oil mixture, and set aside.

Par-cook the bacon strips in the microwave in batches: Put a paper towel on a plate, lay the bacon on top in a single layer, and then cover with another paper towel. Cook on high for 4 to 5 minutes until the strips are translucent but not crispy. Let cool a little. Wrap the strips around the scallops in an S pattern, cutting the bacon into smaller pieces if necessary. Carefully thread the bacon-wrapped scallops onto the skewers (3 to 4 per skewer), brush with the olive oil mixture on each side, and grill over medium heat for about 4 minutes per side.

Places to Go

FARM PROGRAMS FOR KIDS

Farm Based Education Association is a relatively new organization whose mission is to join farm-based education programs in an international association. The Board of Founding Partners lists some participating farms around the country; see www.farmbasededucation.org.

To see how schools can connect with local farms with the objective of improving student nutrition and supporting local agriculture, visit www.farmtoschool.org.

CULINARY PROGRAMS FOR KIDS

Young Chefs Academy is a national franchise with more than 150 cooking schools across the country. They offer culinary classes, mini-camps, and birthday parties geared toward kids between the ages of four and fourteen. Classes are divided by age, and there are at least two instructors per class. For locations and other information, go to www.young chefsacademy.com.

Spoons Across America offers a varied menu of inspiring (and delicious) programs for elementary and middle school kids, including On the Farm, a day-long visit to a farm for third to fifth graders, and the Dinner Party Project, where students plan and prepare a dinner party for their families. (Can I sign my kids up for that one?) They've worked with more than ten thousand public school students across the country since 1995. For more go to spoonsacrossamerica.org.

HISTORIC COOKING AND AGRICULTURAL PROGRAMS

There are living history and agricultural museums across the country. Here is a complete listing, by state. For further information, go to Association for Living History, Farm and Agricultural Museums (www .alhfam.org). Also, check out historian Sandra Oliver's Web site, Food History News (www.foodhistorynews.com).

ALABAMA

Burritt on the Mountain
Huntsville, AL
(256) 536-2882
www.burrittonthemountain.com

Landmark Park
Dothan, AL
(334) 794-3452
www.landmarkpark.com

Peinhardt Living History Farm
Cullman, AL
(256) 734-0850
www.prn-inc.net/peinhardtliving
  historyfarm/history.htm

ARIZONA

Sharlot Hall Museum
Prescott, AZ
(928) 445-3122
www.sharlot.org/events/
  livinghistory/index.html

CALIFORNIA

Ardenwood Historic Farm
Fremont, CA
(510) 796-0199
www.ebparks.org/parks/ardenwood

Blue Ox
Eureka, CA
(800) 248-4259
www.blueoxmill.com

Columbia—Gold Mining Town
Columbia, CA
(209) 536-1672
www.columbiacalifornia.com

Los Encinos State Historic Park
Encino, CA
(818) 784-4849
www.los-encinos.org

Stagecoach Museum
Newbury Park, CA
(805) 498-9441
www.stagecoachmuseum.org

Workman and Temple Family
  Homestead Museum
City of Industry, CA
(626) 968-8492
www.homesteadmuseum.org

COLORADO

Clear Creek History Park and Astor
  House and Museum
Golden, CO
(303) 278-3557
www.astorhousemuseum.org

MacGregor Ranch
Estes Park, CO
(970) 586-3749
www.macgregorranch.org

Rockledge Ranch
Colorado Springs, CO
(719) 578-6777
www.rockledgeranch.com

CONNECTICUT

Mystic Seaport—The Museum of
America and the Sea
Mystic, CT
(860) 572-5315 or (888) 973-2767
www.mysticseaport.org

DELAWARE

Delaware Agricultural Museum and
Village
Dover, DE
(302) 734-1618
www.agriculturalmuseum.org

Hagley Museum and Library
Wilmington, DE
(302) 658-2400
www.hagley.lib.de.us

FLORIDA

Cracker Country
Tampa, FL
(813) 627-4225
www.crackercountry.org

Morningside Living History Farm
Gainesville, FL
(352) 393-8756 or (352) 334-3326.
www.cityofgainesville.org/no

GEORGIA

Westville Village
Lumpkin, GA
(888) 733-1850 or (229) 838-6310
www.westville.org

HAWAII

Kona Historical Society
Captain Cook, HI
(808) 323-3222
www.konahistorical.org/tours

Mission Houses Museum
Honolulu, HI
(808) 531-0481
www.missionhouses.org

IDAHO

R Lucky Star Ranch Farm Tools
Museum
Marsing, ID
www.rluckystarranch.com

ILLINOIS

Apple River Fort SHS
Elizabeth, IL
(815) 858-2028
www.appleriverfort.org/main/
index2.cfm

Garfield Farm
between Geneva and Elburn, IL
(630) 584-8485
www.garfieldfarm.org

Homestead Prairie Farm
Decatur, IL
(217) 423-7708
www.maconcountyconservation
.org/historic.htm

Kline Creek Farm
Winfield, IL
(630) 933-7200
www.dupageforest.com/
EDUCATION/klinecreek.html

Naper Settlement
Naperville, IL
(630) 420-6010
www.napersettlement.org

INDIANA

Conner Prairie
Fishers, IN
(317) 776-6000
www.connerprairie.org

Museum at Prophetstown
Battle Ground, IN
(765) 567-4700
www.prophetstown.org

Skinner Farm Village
Perrysville, IN
www.skinnervillage.eshire.net

IOWA

Living History Farms
Urbandale, IA
(515) 278-5286
www.lhf.org

KANSAS

National Agricultural Hall of Fame
Bonner Springs, KS
(913) 721-1075
www.aghalloffame.com

Old Cowtown Museum
Witchita, KS
(316) 660-1864
www.oldcowtown.org

LOUISIANA

Hermann-Grima/Gallier Historic
    Houses Administrative Office
New Orleans, LA
(504) 525-5661
www.hgghh.org

Louisiana State University Rural
    Life Museum
Baton Rouge, LA
(225) 765-2437
www.rurallife.lsu.edu

Kent Plantation House
Alexandria, LA
(318) 487-5998
www.kenthouse.org

Melrose Plantation
Melrose, LA
(318) 379-0055
www.preservenatchitoches.org

MAINE

Washburn-Norlands Living History
    Center
Livermore, ME
(207) 897-4366
www.norlands.org

Willowbrook Museum Village
Newfield, ME
(207) 793-2784
www.willowbrookmuseum.org

MARYLAND

Historic St. Mary's City
St. Mary's City, MD
(800) 762-1634, (240) 895-4990, or
(240) 895-4960
www.stmaryscity.org

Kinder Farm Park
Millersville, MD
(410) 222-6115
http://www.aacounty.org/
RecParks/parks/kinderfarm_park

MASSACHUSETTS

Hancock Shaker Village
Pittsfield, MA
(413) 443-0188 or (800) 817-1137
www.hancockshakervillage.org

Historic Deerfield
Deerfield, MA
(413) 775-7214
www.historic-deerfield.org

Old Sturbridge Village
Sturbridge, MA
(800) SEE-1830 or (508) 347-3362
www.osv.org

Plimoth Plantation
Plymouth, MA
(508) 746-1622
www.plimoth.org

MICHIGAN

Greenfield Village
Dearborn, MI
(313) 982-6001 or (800) 835-5237
www.hfmgv.org/village/default.asp

Mackinaw State Historic Park
Mackinaw City, MI
(231) 436-4100
www.mackinacparks.com

MINNESOTA

Farm America
Waseca, MN
(507) 835-2052
www.farmamerica.org

MISSOURI

Missouri Town 1855
Blue Springs, MO
(816) 503-4860
www.jackson.org (click on
Recreation and then click on
Historic Site)

Watkins Mill
Lawson, MO
(816) 580-3387
www.watkinsmill.org

MONTANA

Montana Heritage Commission
Virginia City, MT
(800) 829-2969
www.virginiacitymt.com/
LivHistory.asp

NEBRASKA

North Platte Valley Museum
Gering, NE
(308) 436-5411
www.npvm.org

Stuhr Museum of the Prairie
 Pioneer
Grand Island, NE
(308) 385-5316
www.stuhrmuseum.org

NEW HAMPSHIRE

Enfield Shaker Museum
Enfield, NH
(603) 632-4346
www.shakermuseum.org

Fort at No. 4 Living History Museum
Charleston, NH
(603) 826-5700
www.fortat4.com

Heritage New Hampshire
Glen, NH
(603) 383-4186
www.heritagenh.com

Remick Country Doctor Museum
 & Farm
Tamworth, NH
(603) 323-7591 or (800) 686-6117
www.remickmuseum.org

Strawbery Banke Museum
Portsmouth, NH
(603) 433-1100
www.strawberybanke.org

NEW JERSEY

Historic Cold Spring Village
Cape May, NJ
(609) 898-2300
www.hcsv.org

Howell Living History Farm
Lambertsville, NJ
(609) 737-3299
www.howellfarm.com

Old Barracks Museum
Trenton, NJ
(609) 396-1776
www.barracks.org

Victorian Cape May NJ
Mid-Atlantic Center for the Arts
Cape May, NJ
(609) 884-5404 or (800) 275-4278
www.capemaymac.org/index
 .html

NEW MEXICO

El Rancho de las Golondrinas
Santa Fe, NM
(505) 471-2261
www.golondrinas.org

New Mexico Farm and Ranch
 Heritage Museum
Las Cruces, NM
(505) 522-4100
www.nmfarmandranchmuseum-
 .org

NEW YORK

Erie Canal Museum
Syracuse, NY
(315) 471-0593
www.eriecanalmuseum.org

Farmers' Museum
Cooperstown, NY
(607) 547-1450 or (888) 547-1450
www.farmersmuseum.org/farmers

Fort Ticonderoga National Historic
  Landmark
Ticonderoga, NY
(518) 585-2821
www.fort-ticonderoga.org

Genesee Country Village and
  Museum
Mumford, NY
(585) 538-6822
http://www.gcv.org

Hanford Mills Museum
East Meredith, NY
(607) 278-5744
www.hanfordmills.org

Historic Hudson Valley
Tarrytown, NY
(914) 631-8200
www.hudsonvalley.org

Historic Richmond Town
Staten Island, NY
(718) 351-1611
www.historicrichmondtown.org

Lower East Side Tenement Museum
New York, NY
(212) 431-0233
www.tenement.org

Museum Village
Monroe, NY
(845) 782-8248
www.museumvillage.org

Newark Valley Historical Society
Newark Valley, NY
(607) 642-9516
www.nvhistory.org

Ward W. O'Hara Agricultural
  Museum
Auburn, NY
(315) 252-7644
www.cayuganet.org/agmuseum

NORTH CAROLINA

Historic Latta Plantation
Huntersville, NC
(704) 875-2312
www.lattaplantation.org

Old Salem Museums and Gardens
Salem, NC
(888) 653-7253
www.oldsalem.org

Tannenbaum Historic Park
Greensboro, NC
(336) 545-5315
www.greensboro-nc.gov/
  Departments/Parks/facilities/
  tannenbaum

Tryon Palace Historic Sites and
    Gardens
New Bern, NC
(800) 767-1560 or (252) 514-4900
www.tryonpalace.org

OHIO

Hale Farm and Village
Bath, OH
(330) 666-3711
www.wrhs.org/halefarm

Ohio Village
Columbus, OH
(614) 297-2300
www.ohiohistory.org/places/ohvillag

Sauder Village
Archbold, OH
(800) 590-9755
www.saudervillage.org

OREGON

Hanley Farm
Between Jacksonville and Central
    Point, OR
(541) 773-6536
www.sohs.org

PENNSYLVANIA

Bartram's Garden
Pre-Revolutionary Garden and
    Farm of John Bartram
Philadelphia, PA
(215) 729-5281
www.bartramsgarden.org

Colonial Pennsylvania Plantation
Ridley Creek State Park
Media, PA
(610) 566-1725
www.colonialplantation.org

Erie County Historical Society
    Battles Museums of Rural Life
Erie, PA
(814) 454-1813
www.eriecountyhistory.org

Graeme Park Historic Site
Horsham, PA
(215) 343-0965
www.ushistory.org/graeme

Hope Lodge Museum
Fort Washington, PA
(215) 646-1595
www.ushistory.org/hope

Landis Valley Museum
Lancaster, PA
(717) 569-040
www.landisvalleymuseum.org

Meadowcroft Rockshelter Museum
    and Rural Life
Avella, PA
(742) 587-3412
meadowcroft.pghhistory.org

Quiet Valley Living Historical Farm
Stroudsburg, PA
(570) 992-6161
www.quietvalley.org

Roth Living Farm Museum of
   Delaware Valley College
North Wales, PA
(215) 699-3994
www.delval.edu/roth/location.htm

Rough and Tumble Engineers
   Historical Association
Kinzers, PA
(717) 442-4249
www.roughandtumble.org

SOUTH CAROLINA

Historic Brattonsville
Culture and Heritage Museums
Rock Hill, SC
(803) 329-2121
www.chmuseums.org

SOUTH DAKOTA

South Dakota State Agricultural
   Heritage Museum
Brookings, SD
(605) 688-6226
www.agmuseum.com

TEXAS

Barrington Living History Farm
Washington, TX
(936) 878-2214
www.tpwd.state.tx.us/spdest/
   findadest/parks/barrington
   _farm

Buffalo Gap Historic Village
Buffalo Gap, TX
(325) 572-3365
www.buffalogap.com

Dallas History Village
Dallas, TX
(214) 421-5141
www.oldcitypark.org

George Ranch Historical Park
Richmond, TX
(281) 545-9212 (local) or
   (281) 343-0218 (metro)
www.georgeranch.org

Liendo Plantation
Hempstead, TX
(979) 826-3126
www.liendo.org

Log Cabin Village
Fort Worth, TX
(817) 392-5881
www.logcabinvillage.org

Mayborn Museum Complex
Waco, TX
(254) 710-1110
www.baylor.edu/mayborn

National Ranching Heritage Center
Lubbock, TX
(806) 742-0498
www.depts.ttu.edu/ranchhc/home
   .htm

Pioneers Farm
Austin, TX
(512) 837-1215
www.pioneerfarms.org

Sam Houston Memorial Museum
Huntsville, TX
(936) 294-1832
www.shsu.edu

Sauer Beckmann Farmstead at the
    Lyndon B. Johnson State Park
Stonewall, TX
(830) 644-2252
www.tpwd.state.tx.us/spdest/
    findadest/parks/lyndon_b
    _johnson/#sch

VERMONT

Billings Farm and Museum
Woodstock, VT
(802) 457-2355
www.billingsfarm.org

Shelburne Museum
Shelburne, VT
(802) 985-3346
www.shelburnemuseum.org

VIRGINIA

Claude Moore Memorial Farm at
    Turkey Run
McLean, VA
(703) 442-7557
www.1771.org

Colonial Williamsburg Foundation
Williamsburg, VA
(757) 229-1000
www.history.org

Frontier Culture Museum of Virginia
Staunton, VA
(540) 332-7850
www.frontier.virginia.gov

Frying Pan Farm Park
Fairfax, VA
(703) 324-8702
www.fairfaxcounty.gov

Monticello and the Thomas
    Jefferson Foundation
Charlottesville, VA
(434) 984-9822
www.monticello.org

Old City Cemetery
Lynchburg, VA
(434) 847-1465
www.gravegarden.org

Pamplin Historical Park and the
    National Museum of the Civil
    War
Petersburg, VA
(804) 861-2408 or 877-PAMPLIN
    (877-726-7546)
www.pamplinpark.org/hart.html

WASHINGTON

Fort Walla Walla Museum
Walla Walla, WA
(509) 525-7703
www.fortwallawallamuseum.org

Pomeroy Living History Farm
Yacolt, WA
(360) 686-3537
www.pomeroyfarm.org

WEST VIRGINIA

Harpers Ferry, WV
(304) 535-6029
www.nps.gov/hafe

WISCONSIN

Old World Wisconsin
Eagle, WI
(262) 594-6300
www.wisconsinhistory.org/oww

Stonefield
Cassville, WI
(608) 725-5210
www.wisconsinhistory.org/
stonefield

Wade House
Greenbush, WI
(920) 526-3271
www.wisconsinhistory.org/
wadehouse

Australia
www.alhfam.org/index.php?cat_id=212&nav_tree=153,146,212

Canada
www.alhfam.org/index.php?cat_id=210&nav_tree=153,146,210

Europe
www.alhfam.org/index.php?cat_id=211&nav_tree=153,146,211

ANDREW POCKROSE

BESTY BLOCK has written food features and restaurant reviews for the *Boston Globe* and *Wondertime Magazine* and online for NPR's Kitchen Window and Epicurious.com. She lives in Boston with her family. This is her first book.

"If your head spins with all the nutrition advice out there . . . take this humorous, informative journey with Betsy Block. She helps sort it all out and gives you the real-mom bottom line on what you can do to make changes. Best of all, she keeps you laughing all the while."

— **ELLIE KRIEGER,** host of the Food Network's *Healthy Appetite* and author of *The Food You Crave*

A harried married mother of two, Betsy Block is in pursuit of the perfect family meal: local, toxin-free, humane, and healthful. But soon she finds herself in a mealtime maze beset by conflicting, often unrealistic advice, and further complicated by two picky kids and a finicky husband. Determined not to give up the good-food fight, she comes up with a creative ten-step makeover plan. She consults experts, visits farms, and overcomes the pitfalls, struggles, and triumphs of eating well when busy schedules, surreptitious lunch trades, snack machines, permissive grandparents, and willful temptations intervene.

As entertaining as it is informative, *The Dinner Diaries* is for any family who wants to change the way they eat—one forkful at a time.

"It's one thing to cook healthy for yourself, but add two opinionated kids, a husband, and a full schedule, and it really becomes a challenge. Betsy Block has done an amazing job of giving creative tips and nutritional information and relating her adventures on the road to feeding her family in a more healthful way. The book is funny, honest, and full of excellent advice that any mother will appreciate."

— **NELL NEWMAN,** President, Newman's Own Organics

Includes charts, food lists, recipes, tips, and suggested culinary and farm programs for kids.

Visit author Web site: www.dinnerdiaries.com

♻ Printed on recycled stock with 30% post-consumer content.

ALGONQUIN BOOKS

a division of Workman Publishing

225 Varick St., New York, NY 10014

www.algonquin.com

ISBN-13: 978-1-56512-570-4 $14.95
Bookland EAN

51495>

9 781565 125704

© 2008 Algonquin Books of Chapel Hill   Design: Anne Winslow   Illustration: Laura Williams